# WILLIAM BECKFORD
# OF FONTHILL

Frontispiece
to the 1815 Edition of
VATHEK

# WILLIAM BECKFORD OF FONTHILL,

*1760-1844*

## *BICENTENARY ESSAYS*

edited by

**FATMA MOUSSA MAHMOUD**

KENNIKAT PRESS
Port Washington, N. Y./London

WILLIAM BECKFORD OF FONTHILL

First published in 1960
Reissued in 1972 by Kennikat Press
Library of Congress Catalog Card No: 70-159709
ISBN 0-8046-1634-5

Manufactured by Taylor Publishing Company   Dallas, Texas

# CONTENTS

| | Page |
|---|---|
| **ANDRE PARREAUX** | |
| The Caliph and The Swinish Multitude | 1 |
| **BOYD ALEXANDER** | |
| The Decay of Beckford's Genius | 17 |
| **GEOFFREY BULLOUGH** | |
| Beckford's Early Travels and His 'Dream of Delusion' | 31 |
| **MAGDI WAHBA** | |
| Beckford, Portugal and "Childish Error" | 51 |
| **FATMA MOUSSA MAHMOUD** | |
| Beckford, *Vathek* and The Oriental Tale | 63 |
| **MAHMOUD MANZALAOUI** | |
| Pseudo-Orientalism In Transition : The Age of *Vathek* | 123 |
| Catalogue of William Beckford Bicentenary Exhibition at Yale : | |
| A Review | 151 |
| **NOTE ON CONTRIBUTORS** | 159 |

# FOREWORD

The bicentenary of William Beckford is now celebrated in three continents. From France, a scholarly tribute in the form of A. Parreaux' great work, *William Beckford, Auteur de 'Vathek', Etude de la Création Littéraire* (Paris, 1960), is indeed a worthy monument to the years of the Caliph's rhapsodic youth.

From U.S.A. a Bicentenary Exhibition at Yale University Library commemorates the many-sided interests of the polished millionnaire. The Exhibition was opened on the 12th October, 1960 with a lecture from Mr. Boyd Alexander the leading English Beckford scholar.

From Cairo — standing as we do with one foot in the East and another in the West — we send forth our modest contribution, which we have tried to render as cosmopolitan as lay in our power. We offer our readers the concerted efforts of contributors of varied nationalities in tribute to the memory of a highly gifted individual whose wide scope of interests knew no boundaries.

F. M. M.

# THE CALIPH AND THE SWINISH MULTITUDE

by

## ANDRE PARREAUX

> ... learning will be cast into the mire,
> and trodden down under the hoofs of
> a swinish multitude.
> (Edmund Burke, *Reflections on the Revolution in France*, 1790).

*Modern Novel Writing, or the Elegant Enthusiast* was published in 1796, while two editions of *Azemia* appeared in 1797 and 1798. The former work was translated into German in 1798, the latter in French, but not until 1808. *Modern Novel writing* was published under the pseudonym of 'Lady Harriet Marlow', *Azemia* under that of 'Jacquetta Agneta Mariana Jenks'. Of the circumstances of their composition, nothing is known. In Beckford's lifetime they were ascribed either to Robert Merry [1] or to the novelist Charlotte Smith. In fact, were it not for the testimonies of Samuel Rogers, Thomas Moore and Cyrus Redding, we might doubt Beckford's authorship. But the contents of the two books are amply sufficient, as we shall see, to account for Beckford's silence about them. A copy of *Modern Novel Writing* in his own library was inscribed : "W.B. Presentation copy from the divine authoress". And Beckford, with his

---

[1] Robert Merry (1755-1798), who published poems under the name of "Della Crusca", and wrote some epigrams on Pitt and his friends, was a man of advanced ideas, a fact which lent apparent support, in the eyes of the contemporary public, to the ascription to him of Beckford's novels. *Modern Novel Writing* was ascribed to Merry by a reviewer in the *Monthly Magazine* (III (1797), 47), and Mrs. Thrale-Piozzi echoed the rumour that *Azemia* was his work (*Thraliana, The Diary of Mrs. Hester Lynch Thrale*, ed. K.C. Balderston; Oxford, 1942; 2nd ed., 1951, pp. 1061-2).

ambiguous tastes, may have derived some additional pleasure from the use of a feminine disguise.

According to Thomas Moore, the two novels were parodies on the productions of Beckford's half-sister, Elizabeth Hervey; but Moore's assertion is not very convincing, since his mistakes in the spelling of *Azemia* and in the description of the book betray his lack of familiarity with it (²). Beckford himself, at the end of *Azemia,* has given a list of the authors parodied, among whom we find the names of Fanny Burney, Mrs. Radcliffe, Mary Robinson, Mrs. Gunning, Mrs. Inchbald, Helen-Maria Williams, etc... In any case we do not think that the identification of the authors parodied matters very much. The reader of 1960 is still able to take an interest in Jane Austen's parody on the Gothic novel, because the Gothic novel itself has not lost all interest in his eyes. But what Michael Sadleir used to call "the rhapsodical romance of the Lydia Languish kind", which is the main butt of Beckford's parody, awakens little interest outside a narrow circle of scholars and experts, whose professional duty it is to read the *Mistakes of the Heart* or the *Tears of Sensibility*. It is significant that, when Beckford meant to parody the Gothic tale, he was unable to sustain this parodic intention very long. The Gothic episode of over a hundred pages that he inserted into *Azemia* is a striking example of this. It is entitled "ANOTHER BLUE-BEARD! AN AUTHENTIC HISTORY WELL KNOWN IN LINCOLNSHIRE". Although in some respects it recalls Mrs. Radcliffe's manner, it differs from it in that it leaves the supernatural unexplained. On the whole it is a good thrilling story, in which Beckford shows real skill in creating an atmosphere of suspense and terror. (³) No parodic intention is apparent, either in it or

---

(2) Thomas Moore, *Memoirs, Journals, and Correspondence*, London, 1853-56, II, 197.

(3) This absence of parodic intention did not escape the contemporary critic who wrote that the tale of *Blue-Beard* could not be "meant as a jeer on Mrs. Radcliffe... It has all the marks of intentional seriousness..." *(The Monthly Visitor, and Pocket Companion*, II (1797), 85).

in another tale which was prefixed by the author to the second edition of *Azemia* : "Edward and Ellen" has only 27 pages and verges on the sentimental rather than on the Gothic proper. Its most prominent feature is its democratic inspiration. A similar tendency could be detected in the Gothic episode, but here it is much more striking. Edward is a young man who commits a theft to support his wife and their baby ; he is sentenced to fourteen years' deportation to Botany Bay, but Ellen is not allowed to go with him. She is told that, if she also committed a theft, she would be deported with him. Accordingly she steals a piece of muslin from a shop; but, as it is worth more than forty shillings, she is sentenced to death. In his passage to Australia, Edward, who has heard of this, throws himself overboard and is drowned. "Reader !" Beckford concludes, "if thou art of superior rank, give a sigh to the evils occasioned by civilised society, and ask thyself whether forty shillings should be the price of human life ?" The general tendency of the tale is democratic and humanitarian, and more akin in spirit to some novels of the French writer Victor Hugo than to the more conventional stories of Hannah More.

Even in *Modern Novel Writing* there is little parody, and a great deal of nonsense. But this nonsense is not devoid of significance. Listen, for example, to Lord Mahogany's ravings, when he is in the throes of his death agony :

> 'My dear woman', said he, 'had you but lighted the fire in time, we might have gone to Banbury in a nut-shell — but O ! this cursed war — I voted for it — how it burns my brain.'

And he goes on :

> 'Let me measure the moon', said he, 'tis full of marrow, faugh ! but O this torrent of lobsters — stop them, they curl the Heavens. Bottle up the war in a cornfield, and put my vote in hell. Hold me — the room is in flames, and the castle totters, what a serpent is the minister, he has stung mankind — I am a crocodile'.

Would it be an exaggeration to say that Lord Mahogany's delirium is not without method ? *I might have given my vote for peace! but O! 'twas war, war, war! how they bleed! thousands, ten thousands dead! ...O! this cursed war — I voted for it — how it burns my brain... O! conscience, conscience! the troops march — alas! — the war is mine... Bottle up the war in a corn-field, and put my vote in hell...* All this refers obviously to the war against the French Revolution, which was then going on, and to which Beckford tried to put an end by private negotiations through his agents and friends in Paris. This episode, and the failure of Beckford's attempt — apparently through Pitt's enmity — are too well-known to be retold here.[4] What is remarkable perhaps is that Beckford's opposition to the government's policy of war against France separated him from the other Jamaican landlords, who supported it. Lord Mahogany's remorse for having voted for war needs no comment. [5] But his fits of delirium with lucid intervals may be a caricature of George III's intermittent madness. Many of the supporters of Pitt's policy find a place in *Modern Novel Writing* : Henry Dundas, George Rose, William Windham, and also that "immaculate Mr. Reeves", famous for founding an *Association for Preserving Liberty and Property against Levellers and Republicans.* The suspension of the *Habeas Corpus* Act and the enacting of the two Bills against *Treasonable Practices* and *Seditious Meetings* (Nov. 1795) was described by Beckford as "the Act for General Silence", which had made England "the Island of Mum". And the literary supporters of Pitt, William Gifford and *The British Critic,* were addressed by the supposed authoress of *Modern Novel Writing* in the following sarcastic fashion :

> To your virtues, liberality, and candour, the whole nation can bear testimony, for I defy the most impudent of your detractors to shew a single instance amongst all your writings, where you have spoken favorably of any

---

(4) See Guy Chapman, *Beckford*, London, 1952, pp. 259-261.

(5) This may be a reference to Grey's motion in favour of peace (put forward on February 15th, 1796) or to similar motions made earlier by Fox, Wilberforce, and Grey himself in the years 1793-1795.

work that was base enough to vindicate the hoggish herd of the people, that was mean enough to object to any measures of the present wise and incorruptible administration, or that was cowardly enough to censure the just and necessary war in which the nation is now so fortunately engaged. No, ye worthy magistrates of the mind! you have exerted your civil jurisdiction with meritorious perseverance, and if at any time you have stepped forth as warriors to defend the exclusive privileges of the FEW, against the vulgar attacks of the MANY, your demeanour has been truly gallant...

Owing to your animated exertions, and the vigorous measures of your *patrons*, you may soon hope to see the happy inhabitants of this prosperous island express but one opinion, and act with one accord, the rich and the powerful shall be tranquilly triumphant, the low and the wretched patiently submissive, great men shall eat white bread in peace, and the poor feed on barley cakes in silence. Every person in the kingdom shall acknowledge the blessings of a strong regular government...

That your enemies may speedily be cast into dungeons, or sent to Botany Bay, and that yourselves may become placemen, pensioners, peeresses, loan-mongers, bishops and contractors, is the constant wish and earnest prayer of,

    Ladies and Gentlemen,

        Your devoted humble servant,

                HARRIET MARLOW

Other shafts were aimed at some well-known figures. Mrs. Thrale-Piozzi, for instance, was depicted, under the name of Mrs. de Malthe, as follows:

She was fully and properly persuaded that kings can do no wrong, and that they were authorized by heaven to massacre and plunder their own subjects, and to desolate the world at their pleasure. She professed herself the most loyal of all human Beings; was a praiseworthy, orthodox believer, yet with religious enthusiasm she would have doomed all men to the flames, who even suffered themselves to doubt, on any article of faith which she had adopted. For the majority of mankind, who languish in hovels, and wither away by hard labour, she had little compassion. She thought that they were only sent into the world to pay tithes and taxes, and by their incessant exertions to procure luxuries and amusements for the rich and powerful. To be distinguished as a woman of learning, she had ransacked all the indexes of books of science, and of the classics; her writings and discourse were larded with scraps of Latin and Greek, with far-fetched allusions, and obsolete quotations... In her conversation she was frequently lively and sometimes entertaining, and at all times knew better how to please than to attach. She had confirmed all her old prejudices by travelling, and had acquired new ones, and hated a philosopher as much as she feared the devil. (6)

The political tendency of *Modern Novel Writing* is obvious: in it Beckford was taking the side of what he called, in derision of Burke's famous phrase, "the hoggish herd of the people", or, as he was to write in *Azemia,* the "swinish crowds". (7)

*Azemia* is even less of a parody than *Modern Novel Writing,* but as a satirical novel it is far superior. The general theme — a young Turkish girl taken to England and separated from her lover, a young naval officer — is a simple, but convenient pretext to a satire of anti-democratic ideas. Although Beckford sometimes lets himself be carried away by his inborn genius for buffoonery and verbal intoxication — e.g. the list of the guests invited by Colonel Brusque and classified in alphabetical

---

(6) Also the "marquis de Mushroom" may be the Duke of Queensberry — notorious "Old Q", whose residence was, we are told, "the resort of all foreigners of distinction, who had fled from their own country to escape the horrors of liberty", and who, "under his hospitable roof, enjoyed good beef and pudding, eels, mutton cutlets, Irish stew, and pigeon pie, besides strong beer, vegetables and pastry."

(7) By 1797 Burke's phrase, "the swinish multitude" had become a popular slogan. Let us mention, among many other similar productions, Spence's penny weekly, *Pig's Meat, or Lessons for the Swinish Multitude,* and Isaac Eaton's weekly publication, *Hog's Wash, or a Salmagundy for Swine.* A popular collection of democratic songs was entitled *Husks for Swine, Dedicated to the Swine of England, the Rabble of Scotland, and the Wretches of Ireland.*

order from A to W — ([8]) the book is much more coherent than *Modern Novel Writing*.

William Pitt is the main butt of the attack. The *Ode, Panegyrical and Lyrical,* supposedly written by a certain "Mr. Paridel Puffwell, now an under-secretary of state", is worth quoting at some length :

> YE, who places hold, or pensions,
>     And as much as ye can get,
> Come, and hear the praising mention
>     I shall make of Mister Pitt.
>
> All he does is grand and daring,
>     All he says is right and fit ;
> Never let us then be sparing
>     In the praise of Mister Pitt.
>
> Who, like him, can prate down reason,
>     Who so well on taxes hit ?

---

(8) Here is a short typical, fragment of the list:

Aëronauts and Architects, Actors and Archbishops, Alarmists and Auctioneers, Attorneys ; Astronomers and Archdeacons, Accoucheurs and Aides-des-Camp, Antiquarians, and Associates and Agents

Borough-jobbers, Bishops and Biographers ; Booksellers, Botanists, Baronets, and Blacklegs ; Barons, Brewers, Bakers, and Butts.

Critics, Counts, and Calculators ; Chymists, Counsellors, Captains (led) and Contractors ; Curates (rarely) Clerks, Canal-makers and Ciceroni, Conveyancers, Cabinet-makers and Cabinet-ministers.

Divines (dignified), Doctors, Demonstrators, Dukes, Duchesses, and Dancing-masters, (but no Democrats).

Engineers, Earls, Essayists, Election-men and Electors, Ensigns, Encyclopedists, Enclosure-schemers, Electricians, Esquires.

Financiers, Flower-fanciers, Fellows of the Royal and Antiquarian Societies, Fidlers, Flute-players and Faro-players.

Germans, Geographers, Genealogists, Graziers, Gamesters, Generals, Gazette-writers, and Grooms of the Stole ; Gardeners and Guinea-traders, Gaugers and Gunpowder-makers, Heralds, Housebuilders and Histrionic Heroes, Historians, and Hautbois-players and Harpers.

Jews, Jewellers, Improvers, Italians, Jerkers, Jobbers, and Informers.

Knights of the Garter, Bath Thistle, and St. Patrick ; Knights Banneret, Naval and Civil ; and Clerks of the Kitchen and King's Friends.

Who detect a plot of treason
    Half so well as Mister Pitt ?

. . . . . . . . . . . . . . . . . . . . . .

Opposition try to hurt him,
    Only in his place to sit ;
Let *us* not, my friends, desert him,
    Stick ye close to Mr. Pitt.

He the multitude is humbling,
    Britons that doth well befit :
Swinish crowds, who minds your grumbling ?
    Bow the knee to Mister Pitt.

Tho' abroad our men are dying,
    Why should he his projects quit ?
What are orphans, widows, crying,
    To our steady Mister Pitt ?

. . . . . . . . . . . . . . . . . . . . . .

You ne'er see him love a wench, Sir,
    Driving curricle and tit ;
He attends the Treasury-bench, Sir,
    *Sober, honest,* Mister Pitt.

. . . . . . . . . . . . . . . . . . . . . .

Two thirds of that nation starving,
    Now of meat ne'er taste a bit ;
For his friends he still is carving,
    This great statesman — Mister Pitt.

Mister Pitt has elocution
    Greater far than John De Witt ;
Give up then our Constitution,
    As advises Mister Pitt.

. . . . . . . . . . . . . . . . . . . . . .

Britons once were *too* victorious,
    And they love it too much yet ;
Humility is far more glorious,
    As 'tis taught by Mister Pitt.

LO ! fresh millions he will raise, Sir,
    Tho' we don't advance a whit ;
Give him then imperial praise, Sir,
    Viva viva Mister Pitt !

Praise him, all ye Treasury Genii!
    That he's wrong, Oh! ne'er admit;
Fear not Fox's honest keen eye,
    While ye stick to Mister Pitt.

Laud him Bishops, Deans, and Prebends,
    All by inspiration lit;
Praise him, blue and crimson ribands.
    Knights! bepraise your patron Pitt.

Stretch your throats, ye fat Contractors,
    He employs your pot and spit;
Laugh at impotent detractors,
    Envying you and Mister Pitt.

New-made Lords shall join the song, Sirs,
    Nor will Rose or Steele forget
To declaim, or right or wrong, Sirs,
    In the praise of Mister Pitt.

Oh! berhyme him, courtly writers!
    Nares and Gifford, men of wit, (9)
Pye, and all ye ode-inditers,
    Strike your lyres to Mister Pitt!

Learn, each *Jacobin* Reviewer,
    Analytical or Crit.;
Learn from *British* Critics, truer
    To appreciate Mister Pitt.

. . . . . . . . . . . . . . . . . . . . . . . . . .

Obviously the romantic plot matters less than the political satire and Charles Arnold, the hero of the novel, remains a very dim figure. But his companion, Bat Bowling, has more substance and relief. In a way he is the conventional figure of the British sailor, rough of speech and manners, but true of heart and full

---

(9) Robert Nares (1753-1829) was one of the founders of the *British Critic*, and edited the first forty-two numbers of the journal in conjunction with the Rev. William Beloe, whom Beckford satirised in *Modern Novel Writing* as "Mr. Bilbo" (while Nares was mentioned as the "Rev. Mr. Squares"). William Gifford, the author of two satires, the *Baviad* and the *Maeviad*, was entrusted with the editorship of the *Anti-Jacobin* in 1797. H. J. Pye was the Poet Laureate.

of common sense. Here is a sample of his talk while he is dodging the Custom Officers, shortly after landing in England :

> "An Please your honour", said Bat, who could not get the Custom-house Officers out of his head; "an please your honour, I've a heard how this here Gert Britton of ourn is the freeest of all the countries upon yearth, and that there is no let or hindrunce to a man's doing as he wull in no shape whatever. — No:, thinks I, sometimes to myself, why how can that be — when there's ever so much money taken from a man, whether he likes or no ; and then if he does but go for to buy ever so little a matter of counterband goods, whip ! he's in prison ! Now, for my part, I can't think, as I says to myself, where'd be the harm of our trading with folks of other nations, without all that there. I can't say as I likes your forrinners — I knows one Englishman, with beef and pudding in his belly, as the song says, can beat ten Frenchmen : and I dares for to say they always will on the seas, which is our own eilemint all the world over. But then when it pleases his Majesty, God bless him, to give us peace, why I sees no why or wherefore, for not enjoying all the good things of both countries, and all countries beyond sea ; for if they want what we can spare, why not send it them, and take in change what they can spare, and we want, without all this racket of counterband and duties ? Now that's my notion of trade, and I do think it would be better. — What cheap brandy we should have in that case !"

It is true that to a large extent Bat Bowling remains a conventional figure, and a convenient mouthpiece for political propaganda. At the same time, we may overestress the conventionality in his character, if we do not keep in mind what was the state of things at large while *Azemia* was being written.

We must not forget that, when the book was published in July 1797, the naval mutinies at Spithead and the Nore had not been over very long. They started on the 15th of April and ended in June. Some of the documents available, those in particular in which the mutineeers gave vent to their grievances, strike us as not entirely dissimilar, both in content and tone, to Bat Bowling's utterances. This is the strain in which they wrote to the Admiralty :

> Dam my eyes if I understand your lingo or long proclama-

tions, but, in short, give us our due at once, and no more of it, till we go in search of the rascals, the enemys of our country. (¹⁰)

And if we think that Bat Bowling's social criticism has little verisimilitude in a common sailor's mouth, let us listen to one of their songs :

> In days of yore when rich and poor agreed,
> Poor served the rich and rich the poor relieved ;
> No despotic tyrants then the womb produced,
> But mutual all, each loved, and none abused,
> But now how dreadful is the scene reversed,
> We're blest with birth, but with oppression cursed. (¹¹)

But even more than Bat Bowling, Mrs. Blandford is the author's mouthpiece. Being childless and kind-hearted, she decides to adopt Azemia as her daughter. A dialogue in which she replies to a selfish man of fashion affords the author an opportunity for discussing social problems. After attending a party the night before, Mrs. Blandford declares herself shocked

> ...to think, that, while a person like our hostess of last night can, for a few hours amusement, expend a sum that would make families happy for years, there is, within a few miles of her splendid abode, a poor industrious group, a father and mother, and aged grand-mother, and so many children, who are actually liable to perish for want of the mere necessaries of existence ?"...

> "Good God !" exclaimed Mr. Perkly, "it is possible that a woman of your sense — of your understanding, can for a moment, allow yourself to be so misled by the nonsensical clamour of the multitude, as to imagine that a plan could ever succeed that went to universal equalization ?"

> "No, Sir", said Mrs. Blandford coolly, "I do *not* join in that clamour. I know, and so does every body of common sense, that equality, according to the sense you affect to annex to it, cannot exist : but there ought to be equal laws for all men".

---

(10) From the Papers of the Repulse (in Conrad Gill, *The Naval Mutinies of 1797*, 1913, p. 123).

(11) See P.A. Brown, *The French Revolution in English History*, p. 156.

"And *are* there not ?" cried Perkly, eagerly. "Is there a country under Heaven where law is so equally dealt as it is in ours ? Is there no justice to be had for every body ?" "Justice !" answered Mrs. Blandford. "Oh ! mockery of terms ! You may as well say to the wretched pauper who beseeches in the street your charity to relieve his hunger — 'Friend, why are you hungry ? There is a tavern open on the opposite side of the way, where you may eat your fill'. — Would not, this be a barbarous insult to the poor mendicant's distress ? — Yet it is precisely thus people talk who urge to the oppressed in common life the excellence, the equality of the English law... No, never talk, my good Sir, of the equality of our laws, while a Chancery-suit is ranked as an evil of as great magnitude as a fire, an inundation, a descent of the enemy, or an earthquake ; and really as to the ruin they produce, I see but little difference — what difference there is, is rather against a Chancery-suit : the invasion, inundation, earthquake, may render a family houseless and desolate at once ; a Chancery-suit keeps them in lingering misery for years, and leaves them beggars at last."

"Well, well," said Mr. Perkly, who felt, though he determined not to own it, that he had hitherto the worst of the argument ; "well, well, but.... that.... a.... that.... a.... is not.... a.... my meaning. No, no — I mean, dear Madam, *that* equality of property, or, as we say, the Agrarian Law, about which so much nonsense has been talked".

"I do not know", answered Mrs. Blandford, "that it might always be such absolute nonsense, however impracticable it is in the present state of society.... All I mean is, that when the thinking mind is shocked by such striking disparity as between the scene I was in last night, and what I now witness passing in this house, it is very apt to advert to the great nations where such symptoms were the forerunners of dreadful convulsions. It is a disease which we know from repeated experience is fatal : I would prevent its being so here ; I would not have the rich live much worse than they do, but I would have the poor supported a great deal better."

There is no need for us to stress the boldness of such statements in 1797 — particularly the reference to the "Agrarian Law", that bugbear of the propertied classes in those days, when the French socialist Babeuf had just been executed, and Tom Paine published his work on *Agrarian Justice*.

Precisely the years 1796-1798, when *Modern Novel Writing* and *Azemia* appeared, were a turning-point in the attitude of left-wing English writers. Southey's *Hymn to the Penates*, Coleridge's *Ode, to France*, Book XI of Wordsworth's *Prelude*, all bear the mark, in various fashions, of the change which was taking place in their authors' minds — a change which had beeen heralded as early as 1795 by Godwin's *Considerations*. (12) The same evolution was noticeable in those artistic circles, whose leading figures were not unknown to Beckford, from Downman to Romney — Romney who, Farington wrote in 1797, "is a convert from Democracy, and now says He believes 'Monarchy is best after all' ". The political situation in 1797 was thus summed up by William Godwin:

> The societies have perished, or where they have not, have shrunk to a skeleton ; the days of democratical declamation are no more ; even the starving labourer in the alehouse is become the champion of aristocracy....

Jacobinism, Godwin went on, was destroyed, its tenets were "involved in almost universal unpopularity and odium ; they were deserted by almost every man high and low in the island of Great Britain." (13) Under such circumstances, it is quite understandable that Beckford should have chosen to express his subversive opinions under the cover of a pseudonym. Those were the days which Blake described in unforgettable lines :

> Every house a den, every man bound : the shadows are fill'd
> With spectres, and the windows wove over with curses of
> iron :

---

(12) "Towards the end of 1795... while the restraining Bills were being discussed in Parliament, an anonymous pamphlet came out, entitled *"Considerantions on Lord Grenville's and Mr. Pitt's Bills*, by a Lover of Order", in which the campaign of the Reformers was branded as criminal" (Charles Cestre, *John Thelwall*, 1906, pp. 136-7). This anonymous pamphlet was the work of William Godwin, as he himself admitted in his correspondence with Thelwall.

(13) See H.N. Brailsford, *Shelley, Godwin and their Circle*, O.U.P., 2nd ed., 1951, p. 113

Over the doors "Thou shalt not" and over the chimneys
"Fear" is written....

And William Blake, in that same year 1797, did not think fit to express his indignation openly and confined it to the margins of his copy of Bishop Watson's *An Apology for the Bible*. The article which the *European Magazine* for September 1797 devoted to William Beckford might have been inspired, as some of his biographers believe, by the author of *Azemia* himself : if such was the case, the frankness with which he proclaimed his friendly relations with the Revolutionary *Commune* is worth noting. ([14])

To what extent did "Beckford the Caliph" believe in Mrs. Blandford's democratic theories and Bat Bowling's subversive utterances ?

At a time when "men even of respectable characters and honest intentions thought it an heroical act of duty, to watch the conduct of their intimate friends, excite them to utter violent or seditious expressions, and afterwards to turn informers against the intemperance they had provoked", ([15]) it took at least same measure of courage and sincerity to express such ideas even under the precarious disguise of a pseudonym. Of course it is always a delicate task to attempt to assess anyone's sincerity. And people always tend to assume that a person of substance like Beckford could have but little sympathy for democratic ideas. But the greatest and most dangerous pitfall would consist, we think, in simplifying unduly a complex notion. And Beckford's psychology was certainly *very* complex. Anyone

---

(14) "... It is remarkable, that in the passport granted him for his departure from France, soon after the death of the King in 1793, it was declared that the Capital saw him depart with regret — '*Paris la* (sic) *voit s'en aller avec regret*'; an expression of voluntary regard and consideration rarely, if ever, paid to an individual in a similar case..." (*The European Magazine*, XXXII (1797), 149).

(15) *Memoirs of the late Thomas Holcroft, written by himself and continued to the time of his death, from his diary, notes and other papers*, 3 vols, London 1816; II, 150-151.

who has read his *Journal* or his correspondence (16) can hardly fail to realise this. We have attempted elsewhere to give a brief sketch of Beckford's personality as we see it, and in the end we had to use a great many question-marks. (17) In any case if we want to understand something of Beckford's political attitude in 1797, we must take into account not only his desire to play a decisive part in the conclusion of a peace treaty with France, but also the whig tradition handed on by his father the Lord Mayor, and his personal dislike of Pitt. Above all perhaps we must not forget the treatment received from His Majesty's Minister at Lisbon in 1787 (which must have long rankled in Beckford's memory), nor the way he was being shunned by the "good society" of England on account of his notorious sexual reputation. True, even these facts cannot solve the puzzle of Beckford's satirical novels, but they will at least help us to understand why his view, in 1797, did not bear the mark of political orthodoxy, any more than his actions conformed to the accepted pattern of behaviour in the British society of his day.

---

(16) No complete edition of Beckford's correspondence has yet been published. Lewis Melville's *Life and Letters of William Beckford of Fonthill* (1910) is faulty, but still indispensable. Important letters and fragments have also been published in J.W. Oliver's *Life of William Beckford* (1932) and Guy Chapman's *Beckford* (1937; 2nd ed. 1952). More recently Boyd Alexander has edited and translated (mostly from the Italian) a number of letters, which were published in 1957 under the title *Life at Fonthill : 1807-1822* — a fascinating book which throws much light on Beckford's personality in his elder years.

(17) *William Beckford auteur de Vathek (1760-1844). Etude de la création littéraire.* Paris: A. G. Nizet, éditeur, 1960.

# THE DECAY OF BECKFORD'S GENIUS

by

## BOYD ALEXANDER

There are many puzzles in Beckford's life. One unanswered question is : Why was his literary output so small ?

From adolescence he was always scribbling. He had a vivid imagination and was an acute and cynical observer of the human scene. He started off well by writing *Biographical Memoirs of Extraordinary Painters* (an original work, worth attention) at the age of sixteen. ([1]) During his first winter in Switzerland, when just seventeen, he drafted an autobiographical fragment, *The Vision*. ([2]) Next summer he wrote an interesting account of his visit to the monastery of the Grande Chartreuse in 1778. ([3]) When travelling in Italy in 1780 he laid the foundations of his travel-book *Dreams, Waking Thoughts and Incidents*. Early in 1782 he conceived *Vathek,* and perhaps rapidly wrote the three *Episodes of Vathek* which, but for Henley's treachery, would have been published with *Vathek*.([4]) During the same period he was translating freely into French a version of the *Arabian Nights* brought back in manuscript form from the Near East by Edward Wortley Montagu. He was also composing original 'Arabian' tales such as Darianoc. ([5]) In 1787 he wrote

---

(1) I give the proof for this early date (1777) in the Study of Beckford, to be published in 1961 under the title *England's Wealthiest Son*. Beckford's book was published anonymously in 1780.

(2) First published in 1930, by Messrs Constable.

(3) Included by Beckford in his suppressed anonymous *Dreams, Waking Thoughts and Incidents* (1783); with the latter it was reprinted in his *Italy; with Shetches of Spain and Portugal, 1834*.

(4) They were not in fact published until 1912, by Messrs Stephen Swift, with an English translation by Sir F. T. Marzials.

(5) These, and some of his translations from the Arabic, still lie unpublished in his Papers (owned by the Duke of Hamilton).

his day-to-day Portuguese Journal,(⁶) intending much of it for publication — in letter-form, as was then fashionable. This was a promising and fruitful beginning for a young man.

Then a great silence fell. Nine years elapsed before he published his next book, *Modern Novel Writing* (1796) — rather a slender volume, but a clever skit. (⁷) This was quickly followed by *Azemia*, which is tedious except for its interesting and unorthodox political passages. The quality of his work, as well as its quantity, noticeably declines, and *Al Raoui* (translated from the Arabic in 1783) (⁸) and *Epitaphs* (1825) are beneath contempt.

Only in extreme old age (by which time certain passions must have been extinguished) did the smouldering embers of Beckford's creative literary activity glow for a moment. In 1834 he served up the publishable portions of his Portuguese-Spanish Journal of 1787-1788 (with the addition of certain 'letters' drafted at much later dates, and the small diary which he kept at Aranjuez in 1795). (⁹) Encouraged by its well-deserved reception, he then wrote his best work since the Journal — his *Recollections of an Excursion to the Monasteries of Alcobaça and Bathalha (1835)*. This was not merely the re-living of memories of a trip made forty-one years earlier, but a work of imagination and description in its own right.

What were the reasons for this long silence? Why this paucity of production by an inveterate scribbler who began so promisingly? Some reasons are obvious. Beckford had bad luck and early discouragement. In 1783 his family, anxious for his political preferment, persuaded him to suppress his (up-to-then)

---

(6) First published in 1954 by Messrs Hart-Davis and edited by Boyd Alexander. It also covers his first few weeks in Spain up till January 1788.

(7) Anonymous *Popular Tales of the Germans* (1791) is attributed to Beckford. It is a free translation of the German stories of J.C.A. Musaeus, and is very tedious.

(8) Published anonymously in 1799. I give my reasons for attributing it to Beckford in an Appendix to the Catalogue of the Bicentenary Exhibition of Beckfordiana at Yale University, October 1960.

(9) i.e., as Vol. II of *Italy; with Sketches of Spain and Portugal*.

most important and lengthy printed work — *Dreams and Waking Thoughs*. In 1786 Henley's treachery robbed him of the credit for *Vathek* and created the impression that it was a mere translation of an existing Arabian tale. But Beckford had a tough and resilient strain in him, and this adversity would not have continued to discourage him from publication for so long.

His social position did not help him to be a writer, since in those days wealthy and well-connected gentlemen were expected to be dilettanti. But this did not prevent Horace Walpole, for example, producing a good deal; and Beckford had an unconventional outlook. His natural bent towards writing was partly countered by two characteristics — indolence and finickiness.

He himself complains of this 'indolence', which is apparent from the frequency with which his unpublished diary entries and compositions break off, even in mid-sentence. Physically he was a very active man, and his life was lived to a rigid time-table; his days at Fonthill were well occupied in a routine kind of way. He was not, therefore, an idle man; no, it was a creative indolence which he usually means. It was partly due to his spoilt childhood, having too much money and being too easily able to gratify his whims.

Hazlitt noticed the finickiness in Beckford's literary style and in his taste as a collector. He was always correcting his drafts and slow to commit himself irrevocably to print — which drove Henley to despair and was one reason why he published *Vathek* without Beckford's consent. The pair of them were concocting the egregious *Notes* to *Vathek* over a period of years!

From the winter of 1796 Beckford's energies were increasingly diverted to the building of Fonthill Abbey, the creation of a flowering wilderness in the 519 acres behind its Barrier wall, and the collecting of pictures, books and objets d'art. Nevertheless, all these reasons are insufficient to account for the smallness of his literary output during so long and active a life, and its almost total evaporation after such a promising and early start.

His life at Fonthill provides the missing clue. The letters which he wrote from there (often daily, with an occasional 'third edition' on the same day) to his factotum Franchi between 1807 and 1822 reveal his state of mind. ([10]) He told his first biographer, Redding, that he was never bored ; and none of his letters (after 1784) hitherto printed were so private and uninhibited. Often these latter were written with a view to publication, or to semi-official correspondents like Sir Isaac Heard, the Herald. They have an eighteenth-century urbanity ; they give no inkling of the rage that filled Beckford's heart after 1784, of his state of frustration, boredom and unquenched desire. How could a man eaten up by such a canker and living in that vacuum at Fonthill be productive ?

*Life at Fonthill* shows that he lived in complete social isolation there for nearly thirty years after his disgrace in October 1784. The scandal was engineered and spread by a political enemy, who 'framed' him during a house-party at Powderham Castle and accused him of illicit relations with the sixteen-year old William Courtenay, later Earl of Devon. Beckford, still only twenty-four, was robbed of his promised peerage ; no book could ever appear under his own name ;([11]) and he laboured under a sense of grievance as a man unjustly accused and condemned without a hearing (particularly after he was publicly blamed for his beloved wife's death in 1786).

Beckford's struggle with his homosexual tendencies, and the consequent ostracism contributed, then, more than anything else to his literary sterility. It is therefore worth considering the little-known *Episodes of Vathek*, which are thinly veiled

---

(10) Translated from the Italian by Boyd Alexander in 1957, under the title *Life at Fonthill, 1807-1822* They are a selection of the best letters; the rest give a still stronger impression of Beckford's negative state of mind.

(11) This is partly why all his subsequent works ( when not anonymous) are by "The author of Vathek".

autobiography. Two of them trace the development of his friendship with Courtenay and shew its destructiveness and immutable consequences.

Unfortunately, Beckford did not refer to them by name during their composition, so that we cannot date them very closely. But at least one of them was being composed in 1783; a second was well under way by May 1784 and was perhaps finished in March 1785, when a third was started; all three were 'nearly finished' by February 1786. (12)

The first Episode (which may have been finished before the Powderham scandal) is called *The Story of Prince Alasi and the Princess Firouz-Kah*. But the early editions of *Vathek* in French were more honest over the title, referring to it as *Histoire des deux princes amis, Alasi et Firouz* ! As its text stands, Beckford lost his nerve and deferred to his readers' prejudice half-way through by turning Prince Firouz (Courtenay) into his sister Firouz-Kah. But she looks exactly like him, and later dons male attire again !

The story opens with Alasi in a position similar to Beckford's after he had come of age. Alasi is unattracted by the idea of marriage, although he allowed his parents to arrange an engagement for State reasons. All he dares do is to delay his marriage :

> With this almost misanthropic repulsion from the ordinary ways of men, I had to ascend a throne, to govern a numerous people, to endure the ineptitude of the great, and the folly of the meaner folk, to do justice to all, in a word, to live among my subjects.

Beckford was always afraid of being committed emotionally, and so the friendship with Courtenay was at first innocent enough : "Love, which in its own shape would have been repelled, took Friendship's shape, and in that shape effected my ruin," says Alasi. We can understand Beckford's yearning for

---

(12) See *Bibliography of William Beckford* by Guy Champan and John Hodgkin (1930), p. 70. This is an indispensable work.

the disinterested friendship which Courtenay seemed to offer: millionaires are often lonely people, surrounded by sycophants and unable to tell who loves them for themselves rather than their money.

> At last, says Alasi, Heaven has hearkened to my dearest wish. It has sent me the true heart's-friend I should never have found in my court; it has sent him to me adorned with all the charms of innocence — charms that will be followed, at a maturer age, by those good qualities that make of friendship man's highest blessing, and, above all, the highest blessing of a prince, since disinterested friendship is a blessing that a prince can scarcely hope to enjoy.

This childish innocence in Courtenay appealed to Beckford, who was a true Romantic and Rousseau-ite in his adoration of Childhood. He genuinely hoped to shape his character and interests in the right direction.

We even get a disguised account of Courtenay's first impact on him:

> The sound of Firouz' voice, his words, his looks, seemed to confuse my reason, and made my speeech come low and haltingly. He perceived the tumult raging in my breast, and, to appease it, abandoned a certain langour and tenderness of demeanour that he had so far affected, and assumed the childish gaiety and vivacity natural to his years; for he did not appear to be much more than thirteen.

When Beckford married in 1783 he still retained his affection for Courtenay; as Alasi says to Firouz: "What is there in common between the affection I shall owe to my wife, and the affection I shall ever entertain for yourself".

But Firouz became increasingly tyrannical; he was spoiled and arrogant, with an essentially bad heart. Although Alasi perceived this, he was powerless: Firouz "played upon me as he listed. Besides, he had himself well in hand, knew how to act so as to excite my sympathy, and to seem yielding and amenable, as it served his purpose." For an irresistible force compelled Alasi to love him; but he could not understand his feelings, so contrary to reason and good sense: "Friend of my soul, Fate alone can be answerable for the strange and unaccountable feelings of our hearts." Beckford's Byronic sense of Fate was one of his main traits, and partly stemmed from his position in life and society as a homosexual.

Firouz' character is painted black, and he is seen as the corrupting influence. Was it that Beckford turned round and blamed Courtenay for his own fate and his own weakness? All that we subsequently learn of Courtenay, and the portrait of him by Romney in 1793, support Beckford's judgment. In the parallel case of Oscar Wilde and Lord Alfred Douglas, we know that it was the latter who was the corrupter and who exploited his older friend's weakness. Beckford had projected too much upon Courtenay, as he did on every new friend. But long before the scandal he began to perceive his friend's worthless character, and yet could not disengage himself. As early as February 1784 he feared that the most careful tutoring "will not prevent his being a trifling inconsistent character."

The turning point in Alasi's life came when he believed the deceitful youth at a critical juncture, in preference to his fiancée; after that, she was compelled to abandon him to his fate. Perhaps Beckford thought that his own marriage gave him the opportunity to transfer his affections and loyalties in the usual way, instead of shilly-shallying between the two. Then, when he let that golden opportunity pass, he was unable to escape from the net of ambiguous entanglements.

Thus, when Alasi was bound by crime to Firouz, he felt that he could not retrace his steps or take a different road; he had already chosen between God and His ennemies:

> 'O Mahomet!... thou hast forsaken me utterly and without hope! What refuge have I, save with thine ennemies,'
> ...I could not recall the past, probably I should not have recalled it if I could. No course was open to me save to leap, with eyes self-bound into the yawning abyss of the future.

"Without hope', Alasi wails! Beckford too believed in God, in Judgment and Damnation, and was without Hope for himself at the last.

Now, on their way to Hell, the two friends were committed irrevocably to each other:

> It was already night when we came to the Terrace of the Beacon Lights ; and, notwithstanding all that we could say to one another of endearment and encouragement, we were filled with a kind of horror as we walked it from end to end. There was no moon in the firmament to shed upon us its soft rays. The stars alone were shining there; but their trembling light only seemed to intensify the sombre grandeur of all that met our gaze. We regretted, indeed, none of the beauties, none of the riches of the world we were about to leave. We thought only of living in a world where we should be for ever inseparable.

Beckford wrote similarly in 1812 about preferring the company of young pathics "to all goods or titles and to all glory present or future". ([13])

But even this was an illusion. Beckford foresaw that the punishment of those 'criminal souls' was 'the final extinction of every feeling save hatred and despair.' For at the end Alasi says :

> What a god have we served ! What a fearful doom has he pronounced upon us ! What ! we who had loved one another so well, must our love be turned to hate ? We, who had come hither to enjoy an eternity of love, must we hate each other to all time!

Whatever we may think of this as a prophecy of the ultimate outcome of such attachments, the fact remains that these friendships of Beckford's did end in frustration and recrimination.

The third Episode *(The Story of the Princess Zulkaïs and the Prince Kalilah)* concerns the Princess' inordinate affection for her twin brother Kalilah, and her father's vain attempt to separate them. As a forbidden relationship, it corresponds to Beckford's with Courtenay. If the latter was like the Zulkaïs-Kalilah friendship, it was not sexual but purely emotional. The childish dream in which Beckford often indulged in his reveries about Courtenay occurs in this Episode—the desire to take a drug that "will lull us painlessly to sleep in each other's arms,

---

([13]) *Life at Fonthill.* p. 134.

and so bear our souls imperceptibly into the peace of another existence!"

The story opens with a superb sketch of Beckford's father as a buccaneering Merchant-Prince, under the guise of the Emir Abou Taher Achmed. The boyhood of his son, Prince Kalilah, is remarkably like Beckford's. Kalilah's father was over-anxious for him to be outstanding, and subjected him to a rigorous course of study above his years.

The fears and disappointment of the Beckford family during his youth and when he was later dallying with Courtenay are exactly expressed in the story:

> Must the sun, as it rises and sets, see you only bloom and fade like a weak narcissus flower. Vainly do the sages try to move you by the most eloquent discourses, and unveil before your eyes the learned mysteries of an older time; vainly do they tell you of warlike and magnanimous deeds. You are now nearly thirteen, and have you evinced the smallest ambition to distinguish yourself among your fellow-men? It is not in the lurking haunts of effeminacy that great characters are formed; it is not by reading love poems that men are made fit to govern nations! Princes must act; they must show themselves to the world.

We recollect how bored Beckford was by the American War of Independence, and by politics and money in general.

Unlike Dr. Johnson or Gibbon, he could not embark as a literary free-lance in London. He had a large estate which he loved and a family Parliamentary seat, all of which gave him a County position and obligations which he could not shirk. He was therefore expected to shine in the wrong direction—in extravert activities like politics and government, instead of in literature and patronage of the arts. From Beckford's point of view, therefore, his parents' outlook was too narrow—a path from which he must escape if he was to develop in his own way.

In the story, Beckford (now under the guise of Zulkaïs) is encouraged in this rebellion against his family and his forbidden love by a sinister figure who must represent Alexander Cozens. This was the famous artist, who became Beckford's drawing-master at Fonthill, his confidant and chief friend during Beckford's adolescence and youth. Beckford here reveals him as a practiser of magic, a perverted servant of Eblis, who was the Prince of Hell.

The story breaks off unfinished, with one of Beckford's most imaginative and striking pictures, full of Romantic imagery. Zulkaïs, under the guidance of the old man, has descended into Hell in order to join her love Kalilah :

> A solitary taper of enormous size, fixed upright in a block of marble, lighted up a vast hall, and discovered to my eyes five staircases, whose banisters, made of different metals, faded upward into the darkness. There we stopped, and the old man broke the silence, saying, 'Choose between these staircases....'
>
> He <then> disappeared, and I heard a door closing behind him. Judge of my terror, you who have heard the ebony portals, which confine us for ever in this place of torment, grind upon their hinges !...
>
> Suddenly a voice, clear, sweet, insinuating like the voice of Kalilah, flattered my ears. I seemed, as in a dream, to see him on the staircase of which the banisters were of brass... 'Zulkaïs', said Kalilah, with an afflicted air, 'Allah forbids our union. But Eblis.... extends to us his protection. Implore his aid, and follow the path to which he points you'.
>
> I awoke in a transport of courage and resolution, seized the taper, and began, without hesitation, to ascend the stairway with the brazen banister. The steps seeemed to multiply beneath my feet ; but my resolution never faltered ; and, at last, I reached a chamber, square and immensely spacious, and paved with a marble that was of flesh colour, and marked as with the veins and arteries of the human body. The walls of this place of terror were hidden by huge piles of carpets of a thousand kinds and a thousands hues, and these moved slowly to and fro, as if painfully stirred by human creatures stifling beneath their weight. All around were ranged black chests, whose steel padlocks seemed encrusted with blood.

Enough has been said to lllustrate the autobiographical nature of the *Episodes of Vathek,* and their importance as a Beckford document. The strange thing is that long before this, at the age of seventeen Beckford, in *The Vision,* gives an exact picture of his later situation in Fonthill Abbey, cut off from the outside world but unreconciled to his lot. He is describing the superior but depraved beings who degenerated into malevolent dwarfs huddled in the abyss:

> In the profound abyss .... the guilty race awoke to .... all the horrors of conscience. The most dreadful silence prevailed throughout this gloomy space .... Deprived of the gift of speech and fixed to the spot on which they had fallen, each creature imagined himself in an entire solitude. They had formerly heard of the idea of eternity. They thought that dreadful eternity arrived; an endless duration of darkness, solitude and silence, without a single object to divert the gloom of their situation or a being to whom they might have the consolation to complain. A thousand times they wished all the horrors of punishment and least visible, they wished even the cries of tortures to sound in their ears, any degrees of misery seemed preferable to this total inaction; for to a race whose limbs had always obeyed the vivacity of their souls and whose tongues had been accustomed to utter a million of thoughts which crowded their imaginations, what situation can be conceived more painful than this horrid calm of the body whilst the mind, doubly active, ranged over the former period of its existence, burnt to deprecate the power it had contemned, and found itself at once deprived of all the faculties of expression? (p. 52-53).

The loss of their former position inspired them, like Beckford, with malevolent hatred towards mankind, whom they saw as usurpers.

Had Beckford's literary impulse not been crushed at Fonthill by his incessant internal conflict and the weight of boredom, bitterness and remorse, this Gloomy Egoist might have given us a savage novel to equal *Wuthering Heights*.

This, of course, presupposes that Beckford had a certain genius, and that he was capable of sustaining it from within, despite external disappointments. Was this so? Swinburne, in the fairest verdict on Beckford which I know, wrote to Mallarmé:

> I have always pictured Beckford as a most unhappy man, more deeply consumed by malaise, ennui and melan-

cholia than ever his admirer Byron was. This state is sometimes bottled up and simmering, and sometimes breaks out and explodes everywhere in *Vathek* and in all that is told of him, both true and false. To be a millionaire and to want to be a poet—and only to be half a one! To be conscious of something like genius, but to turn out not to be one after all and nothing more than an *à peu près* ! Almost to succeed in finding the path to artistic creation, and then to fall back on one's riches ! All this must make the life of the poet *manqué* something much more gloomy than the Hall of Eblis. (14)

Already, before his coming-of-age in 1781, when his prospects seemed most splendid and his position unassailable, Beckford voiced his self-doubt, his gnawing anxiety : I fear I shall never be .... good for anything in this world, but composing airs, building towers, forming gardens, collecting old Japan, and writing a journey to China or the moon." (15)

A certain dilettantism is hinted at here. Writing even before this, he exactly foreshadowed his later life at Fonthill :

> The pride of Ancestry and a haughty consciousness of his descent (which he strove in vain to dissemble) rendered him obnoxious to the World in general. And finding himself disliked and dreaded, he had retired from court to the solitude of an ancient castle in the midst of his Duchy, where he employed himself in literary pursuits and forgot his ennuis and ill-humours in the cultivation of the arts and the sciences. He was surrounded by poets, musicians, sculptors and designers, who lost and gained by turns the empire of his mind. Sometimes he was enchanted by chimical researches ; another moment, Architecture engaged his attention, and he built lofty Towers in the morisco style, and added magnificent corinthian porticos to the gothic abodes of his Ancestors. When this rage was subsided, the fury of antiquities began to predominate. Every corner of his Domain was first ransacked for medals and tesselated pavements ; then collectors were sent out to explore the

---

(14) My translation of the French text given in Mallarmé's *Oeuvres Complètes*, ed. Mondor and Jean-Aubry, Paris (Gallimard) 1951, p. 1599.

(15) Beckford to the first wife of Sir William Hamilton, our Naples envoy, 2nd April 1781; first quoted in Melville's *Life and Letters of William Beckford*, 1910, p. 105.

## THE DECAY OF BECKFORD'S GENIUS

most remote provinces of the Kingdom in search of rusty helmets, tattered shields, incriptions and broken milestones. Meanwhile, commissions being sent to Sicily and Greece, whole shiploads of mutilated figures were landed at Alicant, and these pagan images scandalously usurped the nitches of the best Saints in the Calendar. When this passion had worn itself out, a violent admiration of paintings succeeded. Nothing pleased the Grandee but the productions of the pencil. He filled his appartments with the works of Raphael, Titian and Julio Romano at an immense expence, and constructed whole suites of rooms purposely to display them. (16)

Beckford is laughing, it is true, at his own extravagances and at those of the aristocratic amateur of the period. But the point is—they were *extravagances* or, in his own words, 'rages', 'furies', 'passions' which 'wore themselves out'. Even in 1780, then, he saw himself as a man of letters rather than a writer, but still more as collector and dilettante.

---

(16) Pages 101-103 of Beckford's unpublished draft of his autobiographical novel *L'Esplendente*. Beckford is describing one of the characters in the novel, the Duke of d'Arcas, a patron of the arts. The large and unformed handwriting of the MS (quoted here by courtesy of the owners, Hamilton & Kinneil Estates) suggests the date 1780 (if not earlier). Chapman and Hodgkin's *Bibliography*, p. 96, mentions two letters of 1784 and 1785 which are not, however, relevant to the dating of the MS. I have repunctuated Beckford's text, which consists of a series of dashes, which do not make for easy reading in print.

# BECKFORD'S EARLY TRAVELS AND HIS 'DREAM OF DELUSION'

by

**GEOFFREY BULLOUGH**

Among the many striking qualities of that complicated and not unlikeable personality William Beckford was his passion for foreign travel, whether at secondhand through reading, or mentally by day-dream, or by actual physical transportation along the roads of Europe and visits in favoured countries. To explore his motives for wandering far and wide and his expression of the excitement it afforded him, is to throw light on the marred mind of one of the last of the great dilettanti and to reveal aspects of the Romantic temper as it flourished between 1780 and 1840.

Beckford certainly spent much time abroad.(¹) In 1777, at the age of 17, he was sent with his tutor Mr. Lettice to stay in Geneva, whence they made excursions to visit Voltaire and to see the Grande Chartreuse. Returning home for Christmas, 1778 he spent that season in festivities with his friends at Fonthill. The tour of England made in the next summer was probably arranged by his mother to prepare him for the responsible career in English society and politics of which she had high hopes, by acquainting him with the varied life of his own country before he embarked on the Grand Tour, then the climactic phase of every gentleman's education. Doubtless his sentimental attachment to William, son of Viscount Courtenay, a boy of eleven years old, which their elders viewed with disapproval, and Beckford's imprudent intimacy with Louisa, the wife of

---

(1) Some of Beckford's movements are still obscure. My account is based largely on the researches of J. W. Oliver and Guy Chapman.

his second-cousin Peter Beckford, made his departure abroad in June, 1780, seem opportune.

Accompanied by Mr. Lettice he took the route Margate - Ostend - Holland - Spa - Bonn - Munich - Augsburg - Innsbruck, and so into Italy where they visited the chief tourist-places between Venice and Naples. At Naples they stayed with Sir William Hamilton, whose first wife (not 'the Nelson', as he called Emma) was a pure, calming influence on the wayward boy. Thence they retraced their route by Rome, Venice, Augsburg to Strasburg and so to Paris where he stayed some time, arriving home in April, 1781. Before his coming-of-age celebrations in September, when he succeeded to a fortune of a million pounds and an income of £100,000 a year, he started to write up his travel notes for publication. By April 1782 he had written Vathek and other oriental tales, but had also indulged at Christmas and after in pursuits of such doubtful morality that scandal had been caused and he was advised to go abroad for a third time.

He travelled like an ambassador. With a large retinue, in three carriages with outriders and frequent relays of horses he went over old ground, through Ostend, Cologne, Augsburg, Innsbruck, Padua, Venice, working en route at his book, *Dreams, Waking Thoughts* and *Incidents in a Series of Letters* arriving in Rome for the Festival of St. Peter (June 29); thence to Naples; to Portici (where he heard of his good angel Lady Hamilton's death), and home by Leghorn, Turin and Geneva.

By the end of 1782 his travel-sketches were in the press, but the book was never published, for his relatives feared that its tone would give colour to the rumours already widespread about Beckford's way of life. His connection with Louisa was broken off soon after he married Lady Margaret Gordon, with whom he spent some time in Geneva and Paris, returning home by May, 1784. Then came catastrophe. After a month spent at Powderham Castle, seat of the Courtenays, accusations were publicly disseminated that Beckford had committed homosexual misconduct with young William Courtnay. The charges were never proved, but Beckford made the fatal mistake of leaving the country, alone, for his wife was expecting a child. She was loyal to him, and he was soon back, to take her and their baby daughter to Switzerland, where they settled in the Château de la Tour near Vevey. A year later, in May, 1786, Lady Margaret died after the birth of a second daughter.

By now Beckford's reputation was so bad that, as he writes, 'while I was stabbed to the heart, the balm poured into my wounds [was] a set of paragraphs accusing me of having occasioned her death by ill-usage.' He took her body home, and the children, then returned to the Alps until January, 1787. He was now pressed to visit Jamaica, where he had immense possessions, but as the time to embark drew near he liked the prospect less and less, for he dreaded the climate and the life there. 'No one embarked even for transportation with a heavier heart.'

He sailed to Lisbon in March, 1787, and having been very seasick refused to go further. He stayed there for eight months, falling in love with Portugal and striving in vain to get presented to the Queen, against the opposition of the British Ambassador, Robert Walpole. He passed on to Madrid in November, 1787, and, after six months, to Paris, whence he returned to Fonthill in Autumn, 1789. Half a year later he was back in Paris where he lived in luxury for some months despite the growing Revolution. 'What care I for Aristocrates or Democrates. I am an—Autocrate—determined to make the most of every situation'. He was in France once more from November, 1791, to June, 1792. when he left for Switzerland, 'just in time to avoid a scene of the most frightful confusion' (the Terror). Travel now became difficult even for a millionaire: 'I am contracting my train as much as possible', he wrote, not surprisingly, for at one time it numbered eighty-seven. He was in France, however, by the beginning of 1793, and in Paris, when the King was executed. He had great difficulty in getting a passport, but arrived home safely in May.

Off again by the year's end, Beckford went to Portugal and lived there for two years, this time achieving his royal presentation, and visiting in June 1794 the monasteries of Alcobaça and Batalha, which produced forty years later his *Recollections* of the occasion. During the next year or so the war prevented his going to Naples to see Sir William Hamilton, and when he finally set sail he was 'chased by a Barbary corsair' and forced into Alicante (Morocco). From there he reached Valencia and so back to Portugal. When he returned to England in 1796 the difficulties of foreign travel discouraged him from further journeys and he turned to building his Gothic Fonthill, where he surrounded himself with a great wall, planted woods, 'sticking them full of hideous man-traps and spring guns that snap legs off as neatly as Pinchbeck's patent snuffers snuff candles' (Letter to Lady Craven). 'If I am shy or savage you must consider the baitings and worryings.... how I was treated in Portugal, in Spain, in France, in Switzerland, at home, abroad, in every region.'

As a Francophile Beckford regretted the war with France, and in 1797, learning from his agent in Paris that the French government was favourable to peace negotiations, he approached the Duke of Portland and William Pitt, only to be rebuffed.

After his mother's death in July, 1798 he returned to Portugal, staying from September to July, 1799. During the short peace he was twice in France (1801-2); and again, after the fall of Napoleon in 1814 and in 1819. These were his last visits to the Continent. Fonthill occupied him more and more, and he had lost his restlessness. In 1818, however, after a visit from Samuel Rogers, Beckford began to consider publishing his travel-sketches, and requested Thomas Moore the poet to prepare them for the press. Moore declined 'to have my name coupled with his', and the letters were not published until 1834, when *Italy, Spain and Portugal,* containing a revised version of *Dreams Waking Thoughts, and Incidents* appeared. The lonely old man, living latterly at Bath among the collections he had made in several countries and by forays to London sales, still liked to talk about the places and people he had seen, and he kept his vigour to the end: 'I am not tired of life, but life is tired of me', he wrote in his 84th year.

Beckford travelled for many reasons: at first because it was the 'done thing' and required of him by his family; but he soon found in the act of travel, the movement, the changes of scene, the variety of contacts, with the possibility of solitude among unknown men in cities, a charm which amounted for some years to a passion. Then there were the beauty of scenery, the historical and literary associations, the pleasures of music and the other arts, glimpses of a religious life into which he could never truly penetrate but which moved him with ephemeral and spurious 'revelations', all the titillation of senses and emotions mingled with an appeal to his satiric humour.

Later, when, anticipating Byron and Shelley, he 'left his country for his country's good', he knew the bitterness of exile, of persecution by gossip and the active malice of the unco'guid and the envious. He yearned to be accepted by the society he often quite sincerely disdained. But the ralisation that he could never take the position in society which he felt was his right even though he might not desire it, kept him restless and unfulfilled until middle age and the obstacles of war curbed his bitter energy and he could find a focus for his ill-directed life in the narrow aim to make Fonthill an embodiment of his many-sided fancy.

What Beckford published about his journeys differed considerably in tone as his motives and attitude changed. Thus the account of his Excursion to the Grande Chartreuse written in 1778 (2) is a careful description of all that he saw, almost devoid of humour but marked by the 'correct' mixture of wonder and terror and enlivened by touches of the Picturesque. As with Mr. Lettice he approached the "narrow valley overhung by shaggy precipices, above which rose lofty peaks, covered to their very summits with wood", he "experienced some disagreeable sensations, and it was not without a degree of unwillingness that I left the gay pastures and enlivening sunshine, to throw myself into this gloomy and disturbed region."

A little later :

The woods are here clouded with darkness, and the torrents, rushing with additional violence, are lost in the

---

(2) Printed in the suppressed *Dreams, Waking Thoughts and Incidents* (1783).

gloom of the caverns below; every object, as I looked downwards from my path, that hung midway between the base and the summit of the cliff, was horrid and woeful. The channel of the torrent sunk deep amidst frightful crags, and the pale willows and wreathed roots spreading over it, answered my ideas of those dismal abodes, where, according to the druidical mythology, the ghosts of conquered warriors were bound. I shivered whilst I was regarding these regions of desolation, and, quickly lifting up my eyes to vary the scene, I perceived a range of whitish cliffs, glistening with the light of the sun, to emerge from these melancholy forests."

In his unpublished private letters at this time Beckford was already indulging the kind of fancies suggested by his 'druidical' reference here. The *Excursion* shows him in control of day-dream, and deliberately seeking the Sublime by allusions to chasms, grottoes, torrents, mists, and gloom shot through by gleams of light. Perhaps this prentice work shows the restraining influence of his tutor.

By the time he wrote *Dreams, Waking Thoughts and Incidents,* Beckford was much more sure of himself and proud to display his effervescent fantasy. This was to be no ordinary travel-book.

> Shall I tell you my dreams? (he began) To give an account of my time, is doing, I assure you, but little better. Never did there exist a more ideal being. A frequent mist hovers before my eyes, and, through its medium, I see objects so faint and hazy, that both their colours and forms are apt to delude me. This is a rare confession, say the wise, for a traveller to make... But... If—be contented with my visionary way of gazing, I am perfectly pleased. (Letter I) (³)

More will be said later of his 'visionary way'. The book was to give almost full scope to his random sensibility; and the

---

(3) *Dreams, Waking Thoughts* &c. was edited by G.T. Bettany in 1891 in *The History of the Caliph Vathek; and European Travels;* more recently in *The Travel-Diaries of William Beckford of Fonthill,* ed. Guy Chapman, 2 vols, 1928.

sensibility he expressed, though overgiven to floating on a stream of emotional associations which took him far from outer objects, was frequently keenly aware of what went on around him, of the sights and smells of city and country, of people's oddities, of his own effortless superiority to the mob, to the connoisseurs, scholars and polite society he encountered aand treated often with the impolite disdain of a spoiled young man of more wealth than breeding.

Editing these letters fifty years later for publication in *Italy; with Sketches of Spain and Portugal* (1834) Beckford diminished somewhat the flow of self-centred fantasy without destroying their essential nature, and readers of the later volume will note a marked difference between 'the tone of the section devoted to Italy, and that concerning Portugal, based on the journal written in 1787-8. (⁴)

In the intervening five years Beckford's mind had been soured by public humiliation, ostracism, and the persecution which followed him wherever English society had influence on the Continent. His wife had died, and in Portugal he was engaged in a struggle to get himself acknowledged as *persona grata* by the royal court. If he indulged his fancy it would be filled with sadness, as he recognised when, after praising the musicians of the Queen of Portugal's Chapel, and describing a morning during which he was 'absorbed by the harmony of the wind instruments, stationed at a distance in a thicket of orange and bay trees' he comments :

> Did I consult the health of my mind, I should dismiss these musicians ; their plaintive affective tones are sure to awaken in my bosom a long train of mourful recollections, and by the force of associated ideas to plunge me into a state of languor and gloom. (⁵)

If he could not avoid giving way to such trains of thought

---

(4) For the original version see *The Journal of William Beckford in Portugal and Spain, 1787-1788*, ed. Boyd Alexander. 1954. For the text as printed see Bettany, *op. cit.*, or Chapman, *op. cit.*

(5) Letter XXI. Chapman, *op. cit.* ii. 84.

he now seldom wrote them down. The Portuguese and Spanish letters are therefore mainly concerned with external happenings, with life on the fringes of the court, the kindnesses and oddities of his hosts, portraits of personages of importance in their day, descriptions of places done in a witty rather than emotional manner. He was still satiric, for as he wrote to Lady Craven in 1790.

> I have beeen hunted down and persecuted these many years. I have been stung and not allowed opportunities of changing the snarling, barking style you complain of, had I ever so great an inclination. (⁶)

He forbore to publish passages in which he inveighed against his great enemy and obstacle Robert Walpole, but he gave many a hostile thumb-nail sketch, of dull, pedantic, or bigoted nonentities, of bad musicians, of tedious talkers, such as the liberal Mr Street, 'abusing kings, queens and princes with all his might, and roaring after liberty and independence'. He gave a brilliant account of the funeral of an aged English woman who had given way to the wiles of the Church on her deathbed (Letter XXIV). Though sometimes irked by the bustle of social life, Beckford came to enjoy it, and describes the convivial parties, the visits to noble houses with their charming, twittering young ladies, in a lively fashion which shows Beckford the Man of the World supplanting the Rousseauan Solitary. This aspect of him cannot be fully treated in the present essay, which is concerned mainly with the Romantic Beckford of the earlier phase.

The young author of *Dreams, Waking Thoughts and Incidents* was not merely a dreamer, nor were his eyes so 'purblind' as he pretended. He was indeed an acute observer of those people and things which he considered worthy of attention, and the pungency which he affected soon became second nature. In his second Letter, complaining of the children in the apartment above who spoiled his sleep he threatened to 'grow as scurrilous as Dr. Smollett, and be dignified with the appellation of the

---

(6) Cf. B. Alexander, *op. cit.*, p. 13.

Younger Smelfungus.' The 'ideal being' loathed whatever fell short of his ideal, whether it was a question of his own comfort, or the cleanliness of a town, or the smells in St. Mark's, Venice, the quality of music or drama played before him, or the lengthy disquisitions of a Flemish connoisseur.

Beckford lacked the sober pleasure in imparting information shown by Patrick Brydone in his *Tour through Sicily and Malta in Series of Letters to Wm. Beckford Esq. of Somerly in Suffolk* (1773), or the agreeable detachment of John Moore's *View of Society and Manners in Italy* (1781), or the wide range of Mrs. Hester Piozzi in her *Observations and Reflections* (1789), which show a sensitive appreciation of Italian urban life and character. He had none of the anecdotal urbanity which his cousin Peter Beckford displayed in his *Familiar Letters from Italy to a Friend in England* (1805). Beckford's aim was not to instruct future tourists but frankly to express the vagaries of his own personality. In an age when rank and privilege often made their possessors caddish, the young Beckford gloried in his own insolence and intolerance. (Later he was to delete many such expressions). On the other hand he was easily humbled by certain kinds of beauty in the arts and nature. In both respects he had something in common with Byron.

Carefully tutored and taught by experts, Beckford was a complacent but impressionable young man when he made his Grand Tour. He had a passion for music, played the harpsichord and the pianoforte well enough to give amateur performances in society, and was found of improvising on piano or organ. An admirer of Corelli and later of Haydn and Jomelli he preferred free flowing voluptuous melody to strict forms such as the sonata. He had no mercy on poor performers even when they were trying their best to please him—witness his slighting remarks on the 'Genoese family of distinction; very fat and sleek, and terribly addicted to the violin', who tormented him in Lucca. Wherever he could he attended the opera but was a stern critic of singing; his idol was Pachierotti, whom he sought out in Lucca and took for a walk which endangered the soprano's health. Pachierotti sang at the coming of age festivities at Fonthill, and remained Beckford's standard of comparison for ever. The opera at Florence he found boring because it was 'addressed to the sight alone', so he 'gave himself up to conversation. Bedini, first soprano, put my patience to severe proof, during the few minutes I attended. You never beheld such a porpoise... You may suppose how often I invoked Pacchierotti, and regretted the lofty melody of *Quinto Fabio*.' (Letter XVII, Oct. 5). His addiction to composers such as Bertoni and Turini and his delight in the singing of Galuzzi (at Fiesso) arose from their power to excite his passions in the manner of Dryden's *Alexander's Feast*, as when 'the Galuzzi sang some of her father Ferandini's compositions, with a fire, an energy, an expression, that one moment raised me to a pitch of heroism, and the next dissolved me in tears.' Like most other things music was an instrument of sensibility.

In discussing the graphic arts Beckford showed less enthusiasm, perhaps because his taste was orthodox and he wished to avoid the usual tourist gush about the sweetness of Raphael or Guercino, the majesty of Michelangelo. On the whole he wrote more about the pictures he disliked than those he admired. Thus he had the current English dislike of the Flemish painters and their realism, whether he was asked to admire "A most sublime thistle by Snyders... so faithfully imitated that I dare say no ass could have seen it unmoved", or the 'Descent from the Cross' in which Rubens displayed "the gigantic coarseness of his pencil". He was however amused by the St. Anthony of 'Hell-fire Brughel' with its grotesque figures, and he admired the landscapes of Berghems and Wouvermans. In Venice he was bored by Tintoretto and Paolo Veronese, and at Florence he was thrilled, like Shelley [7] and others, by the Medusa's head ascribed (wrongly) to 'that surprising genius Leonardo da Vinci'.

In later life Beckford's taste was to develop and be supported by greater knowledge of the problems and processes of painting. Eclectic though he was, he insisted that whatever he put into Fonthill should be the best of the kind. In art he was

---

(7) Cf. Shelley's *On the Medusa of Leonardo*: 'Tis the tempestuous loveliness of terror', &c.

rather classical than romantic. He owned the 'Saint Catherine' of Raphael and Bellini's 'Doge Lorèdano' and four other pictures now in the National Gallery, as well as two Vernets, three Claude Lorraines, and works by Reynolds and Romney. He regretted the way the British Government 'grudges money for the arts'. and the lack of art-knowledge among his fellow-countrymen:

'Ask why Raphael is the prince of painters—they cannot tell you. Now an Italian amateur of the lowest order will explain all this, and more. A just taste for art is a cultivated taste; there is no royal road to it, as too many think there is. (⁸)

When he wrote *Dreams, Waking Thoughts and Incidents*, however, Beckford was at the beginning of his own training, and despite his friendship with the painters Alexander Cozens and his son John Robert, he showed little more than a conventional, emotional view of art. With regard to sculpture his attitude anticipated Byron's, who saw statues as vehicles of artistic genius or of human story. So the Venus de' Medici enchanted Beckford by 'the warm ivory hue of the original marble... and the softness of the limbs'; and the features he admired were those which 'increased the illusion, and helped me to imagine I beheld a breathing divinity.' (⁹) He was so much the slave of the representational idea that—*pace* Lessing—he had no patience with action in sculpture:

'Sleeping figures with me always produce the finest illusion... But when I see an archer in the very act of discharging his arrow, a dancer with one foot in the air, or a gladiator extending his fist to all eternity, I grow tired, and ask, when will they perform what they are about? (Letter XIII).

---

(8) Quoted by L. Melville, *The Life and Letters of William Beckford*. 1910, p. 295.

(9) Chapman, *op.cit.*, i. 142-3. Compare Byron, *Childe Harold*, iv. 49-52. 'There too the Goddess lives in stone, and fills/The air around with beauty; we inhale/The ambrosial aspect, which, beheld, instills/Part of its immortality' &c. Rejecting 'the paltry jargon of the marble mart'. 'We have eyes:/Blood, pulse and breast confirm the Dardan Shepherd's prize.' Contrast what he wrote in prose: 'The Venus is more for admiration than love.'

He entirely lacked that vision of 'the instant made eternity' which inspired Keats in the 'Grecian Urn' : 'For ever wilt thou love, and she be fair!'

The eclecticism which produced his new Fonthill and its collections already appears in his love of the juxtaposition of styles and periods. Thus at Pisa in the Campo Santo he enjoyed "the mixture of antique sarcophagi with Gothic sepulchres" and Giotto's "strange paintings of hell and the devil". The cathedral itself surpassed his wildest dreams by combining Grecian design, Gothic proportions and a general Oriental appearance. The passion for mingled modes sprang from the depths of his personality. It marked the often incoherent substance of his day-dreams and indicated his failure to unify either his imagination or his character.

In his comments on places Beckford sometimes rivalled Smollett in pungency, but he was most original where his fancy was stimulated. He had no great fondness for the Low Countries, for though he liked their 'Quiet and Content' he thought the people ugly and dull : 'All is still and peaceful in these fertile lowlands : the eye meets nothing but round unmeaning faces at every door, and harmless stupidity smiling at every window'. Nevertheless he gave lively accounts of an evening walk in Antwerp (Letter II), the fair at Haarlem (Letter V). He was more excited by the Tyrol, for it provided contrasts between mountain peaks, clouds, flowery meadows, wildness and happy pastoral life which particularly appealed to him. (Letter VIII, July 26). Some of his remarks on Italian places gain in interest for us by their resemblance to the comments of the Romantic poets. Like Byron Beckford was horrified by the Venetians' treatment of their prisoners, ([10]) confined in dungeons below water-level or in the leads (whence Casanova had escaped in 1756). He 'shuddered whilst passing below' the Bridge of Sighs which 'joins the highest part of the prisons to the secret galleries of the palace', and at night expressed his horror, not in verse, but by drawing 'chasms and subterraneous

---

(10) Cf. *Childe Harlod*, iv. Historical Note I.

hollows, the domain of fear and torture, with chains, racks, wheels and dreadful engines, in the style of Piranesei' (Aug. 4).

He was not in Venice during the Carnival, but his account of Venetian life in the Piazza San Marco, in coffee-house and casino, the opportunities for intrigue, the mingling of races, Turks, Arabs, Greeks, Armenians all rubbing shoulders, helps to explain the fascination Byron found in the city, and provides a background for *Beppo*.

On the other hand Beckford shared Shelley's pleasure in airscapes, effects of light and cloud. As he was first rowed in from Mestre, 'an azure expanse of sea opened to our view, the domes and towers of Venice rising from its bosom'.([11]) He recognised many buildings

> innumerable prints and drawings having made their shapes familiar. Still gliding forwards, the sun casting his last gleams across the waves, and reddening the distant towers, we every moment distinguished some new church or palace in the city, suffused with the evening rays, and reflected with all their glow of colouring from the surface of the waters. The air was still; the sky cloudless; a faint wind just breathing upon the deep, lightly bore its surface against the steps of a chapel in the island of Saint Secondo...' (Aug. 2). ([12])

Thousands of other tourists have delighted in this, and in the 'dancing fires' of the lanterned gondolas moving about at night, but Beckford had an unusual power of suggesting the magical union of sound and vision, for instance as an illuminated barge filled with musicians went by. Looking towards the Euganean Hills, 'Scarce one evening have I failed to remark the changeful scenery of the clouds'.

Others since Beckford (notably Heine and Hawthorne) have imagined the old gods surviving in or returning to the modern world. But few have rhapsodised so excitedly (or

---

(11) Cf. also Childe Harold, iv. 2 'Rising with her tiara of proud towers At airy distance, with majestic motion...

(12) Cf. Shelley's sunset in *Julian and Maddalo:* 'Oh! how beautiful is sunset, when the glow/Of heaven descends upon a land like thee,/Thou paradise of exiles, Italy!'

absurdly) as he, when at the first sight of Rome he ran to a marble cistern close by the way,

> poured water upon my hands, and then, lifting them up to the sylvan Genii of the place, implored their protection. I wished to have run wild in the fresh fields and copses above the Vatican, there to have remained, till fauns might creeep out of their concealment, and satyrs begin to touch their flutes in the twilight, for the place looks still so wondrously classical that I can never persuade myself either Constantine, Attila or the Popes themselves have chased them all away. I think I should have found some out, who would have fed me with milk and chestnuts, have sung me a Latian ditty, and mourned the woeful change which have taken place, since their sacred groves were felled, and Faunus ceased to be oracular. Who can tell but they would have given me some mystic skin to sleep on, that I might have looked into futurity ?' (Letter XXII)

Byron once described poetry as 'the sense of a former world and of a future'. Beckford clearly would have agreed with this romantic definition, though his own attempts in poetic prose have often (as here) a slack-twisted air. He went at once to St. Peter's where he sat for fours hours in reverie. Next morning he returned there but all he gives of his discoveries is a wish to get permission to 'erect a little tabernacle under the dome', there to live with his friend and 'take our walks on the fields of marble', embellishing his windows in Chinese style with transparent curtains of yellow silk, 'to admit the glow of perpetual summer'. (13) To such nonsensical irrelevancies Beckford's mind was prone, especially when oppressed; and he *was* oppressed by all that he had read about Rome, and was determined not to write like an antiquary. 'The thought alone of so much to look at, is quite distracting, and makes me resolve to view nothing at all in a scientific way'. Actually he saw surprisingly little.

The Coliseum he found disfigured by chapels, but he liked the ilex and cypress 'springing from heaps of mouldering ruins,

---

(13) Many years later at Landsdown Tower he made a square room beneath the lantern and hung it with orange-coloured drapery.

relieved by a clear transparent sky, strewed with a few red clouds.' He sat down 'on a shattered frieze' to fill his mind with 'stories of ancient Rome', and other 'ideas which chased one another along.' Whereas Smollett thought chiefly of the brutalities of the games ('The Romans were undoubtedly a barbarous people, who delighted in horrible spectacles.') Beckford recalled scenes of triumph, and whereas Byron put aside the modern life which would have interrupted his introspection and his reminiscences of the antique, Beckford's sense of the Picturesque *à la* Salvator Rosa made him describe the 'wretched rabble' on the Palatine Hill,

> roasting their chestnuts on the very spot, perhaps, where Domitian convened a senate, to harangue upon the delicacies of his entertainment. The light of the flame cast upon the figures around it, and the mixtures of tottering wall with foliage impending above their heads, formed a striking picture, which I stayed contemplating from my pillar, till the fire went out, the assembly dispersed, and none remained but a withered hag, raking, the embers, and muttering to herself.' (Letter XXII, Oct. 31)

Oppressed by Rome, and perhaps by lack of letters from Louisa or William Courtenay Beckford stayed only two and a half days there before hurrying on to Naples and the Hamiltons, with whom he attended the theatre of S. Carlo, where 'Marchesi was singing... some of the poorest music imaginable, with the clearest and most triumphant voice, perhaps, in the universe.' He visited Virgil's tomb and climbed a nearby pinetree to examine the grand sweep of the bay and its glittering sea, 'with Caprea rising from its bosom, and Vesuvius breathing forth a white column of smoke into the æther.' His account of a visit to Baia (Nov. 8) might serve as an introduction to Shelley's poems inspired by that region. Nearby at Misenum he took refreshment from an old woman who told him (he claimed) a long, extravagant tale of passion, poison, remorse and suicide. At Pompeii, in the Temple of Isis, 'I fell into one of those reveries which my imagination is fond of indulging'. He imagined himself 'sailing with the elder Pliny on the first day's eruption', and then watching a ceremony 'to supplicate by prayer and

sacrifice, at this destructive moment, the intervention of Isis.'
He was in Rome again in December, looking forward to arriving
home:

> I eagerly anticipate the placid hours we shall pass,
> perhaps, next summer, on the wild range which belongs to
> our sylvan deities... What have we children of the good old
> Sylvanus to do with the miseries or triumphs of the savages
> that prowl about London ? Let us forget there exists such
> a city...' (Letter XXV)

So his travels had done anything but prepare him for public life. The outline just given indeed shows him as a hypersensitive young man of self-confessed 'romantic disposition', but does not suggest the full force of the 'thousand wild conjectures', the 'delightful delirium', the 'Empire of Dreams', to which he all too often surrendered his whole being, and of which his physical peregrinations were frequently merely an occasion.

He saw himself as a creature of Reason and Fancy :

> These two powers are my Sun and Moon. The first
> dispels vapours and clears up the face of things ; the other
> throws over all Nature a dim Haze, and may be styled the
> Dream of Delusion. ([14])

In Beckford's writings at this time Fancy held almost complete sway. For the hothouse-nurtured, fatherless boy everything had become the food of day-dream. His classical reading, the modern literatures made accessible by his talent for languages, his father's house which provided an 'Egyptian Hall' and an 'Indian Apartment', the grounds well-suited to solitary musings or picnics with a few visitors ; all fostered in him a volatile fancy which was not stabilised by any sense of social responsibility. In adolescence he revelled in books of travel and exotic stories to such an extent that no actual contact with other lands could satisfy his febrile imagination. He was essentially a Mental Traveller, an Alastor-type a generation before Shelley depicted that doomed seeker after the ideal.

---

([14]) Melville, *op. cit.* p. 65.

'I have lately committed myself to the guidance of Voyagers, and followed them over vast Oceans to distant Climates where my exotic inclinations are satisfied', he wrote in 1779, but he had already formed the habit of using travel-books as a springboard to fantasy. In Geneva two years earlier he had imagined himself escaping with his correspondent in a long train of motley associations drawn from voyages all over the globe :

> How should I delight to wander with you thro' remote Forests and pitch our Tents by Moonlight in a Wilderness. Then would we observe the Deer bounding over the Lawn and the Goats frisking on the margin of a Stream without a wish to disturb their happiness... Might we not arrive in new Countries by following the course of Rivers and tracing them thro' all their windings to their Source ? Our Barks should be driven by the current of the Stream : never should we steer them, unless we heard Cataracts roaring from afar. Then should we retire into a Bay among the Spice Groves and, felling tall Trees, form a fence to guard us from the Monsters that prowl nightly in the Woods. Thus secured we would visit our Camels and the attendants of our journey... [He describes a friendly meeting with American Indians; then] Am I addressing myself to a Spirit that catches fire at my own Enthusiasm ?... Come then and explore with me the polar Climates of the Westtern Continent... ([15])

The phantasmagoria anticipates remarkably many motifs in *Alastor*, thus pointing to similar processes of thought as well as similar reading between the two writers. As a whole *Alastor* fails, but even there Shelley introduced allegory, thought and characterization lacking in Beckford. Beckford was a Shelley without the saving grace of a mission in life.

When his half-sister Mrs. Elizabeth Hervey told him of her visit to an art-collection, he used it as a starting-point for a long extravanganza about 'the splendour of Chinese palaces' and 'legendary tales... about the Japanese Idols.'

After his return home from Switzerland in December, 1778, he went out in the late afternoon and wandered 'musing

---

(15) Nov. 24, 1777. Melville, *op. cit.* pp. 37-39.

in the Plain before the House which my Father reared,' imagining the trees his brothers, the turf dew-sprinkled by Fairies; and longed to question the rooks flying homeward, 'Over what woods have ye flown . Tell me what scenes ye have surveyed' —in prophetic parody of moods shared by Shelley and Keats. Going indoors for tea, 'my thoughts were wandering into the interior of Africa and dwelt for hours on those countries I love.' Now his fancy forestalled Coleridge in *Kubla Khan* :

> One instant I imagined myself viewing the marble palaces of Ethiopian princes... I was in Africa, on the brink of the Nile, beneath the Mountains of Amara... we arrived at the hollowed Peak and after exploring a Labyrinth of paths which led to its summit, a wide Cavern appeared before us... we entered the Cavern and fell prostrate before the sacred source of the Nile, which issues silently from a deep Gulph in the Rock. Suddenly the spirit of Father *Ureta* brought me swiftly to a Castle with many towers of grotesque Architecture... Here was deposited ancient records and Histories of which the rest of Men are ignorant, poems sung by the Choirs of Paradise, and volumes which contain the sage Councils of Abraham delivered by that Patriarch in the plains of Mamre... Some irresistible Impulse drove me to the extremity of the Lawn, where I recoiled with Horror and Amazement at the sight of a Precipice whose Basis seemed to rest on the surface of our Globe... 'Thou art gazing', whispered a thin airy voice, 'at the Fortunate Mountain of Paradise...' (16)

The whole vision is too long to quote in full. With its rapid transitions, its climax in a sequence of loss, hindrance, grief and falling, it reminds one in structure and tone less of Coleridge's verse than of De Quincey's opium-dreams :

> In vain I attempted to join the beckoning shades, some dreadful pressure chained me to the ground, in vain I called to those I loved ; my lamentations and loud Cries were lost in the gales. How many times did I stretch forth my Arms and attempt advancing—all my endeavours were fruitless... At length I found myself released, and with a violent effort ran or rather flew upon the Lawn; but as I advanced the Forms retreated, a confused murmur of Rills,

---

(16) Melville, *op. cit.* pp. 60-65.

of voices and of Instruments fled before me; the Rocks, the Woods, the prospect seemed in moton, and as it floated away I followed till, impelled by the swiftness of my steps, I shot headlong from the edge of the Mountain and kept falling, continually falling, till lost in immensity. The Horror and amazement of my descent dissolved the Dream. ([17])

What Coleridge and De Quincey experienced with the aid of opium Beckford may have been able to induce in a state of consciously directed reverie. Or did he, like them, take the drug, but without forming a fatal habit? Was opium in small doses his way of escape from the boredom of long journeys into flights of fancy? Does this explain why Morpheus and other sleeping figures attracted him so much in sculpture? Certainly many of the letters written during the first continental visit have characteristics of the *paradis artificiel*. The taking of opiates at that time was both common and respectable. ([18]) But we need not assume it in Beckford's case. 'Such are my phantastic visions and such my flights of fancy when Reason has abandoned it', he commented. He trained himself to day-dream, to let his mind, and his prose, float away on a stream of images.

We must not be too hard on Beckford. These were boyish exercises. Comparison between the private letters and the *Dreams* shows that in writing up his notes for publication he not only developed considerable powers of description and narrative, but kept his effervescent fancy under some restraint. And as the contrast between the Gothic exuberance of Fonthill Abbey and the formal classicism of Lansdown Tower suggests, bitter experience brought Beckford to a tardy maturity in which he saw elegance and strength as more desirable than hasty improvisation. So when he revised in old age the unpublished *Dreams* of his youth in order to combine it with his memories

---

(17) Compare *Confessions of an Opium Eater*, Pt. III, June 1819.

(18) 'De Quincey mentioned as opium eaters, besides himself and Wilberforce, Lord Erskine, the former prime Minister Addington, and Isaac Milner, Dean of Carlisle.' (E. Schneider, *Coleridge Opium and Kubla Khan*. Chicago, 1953, p 33.) Crabbe and Sir James Mackintosh were regular takers of the drug.

of Portugal and Spain, he made many omissions. These included satiric expressions in juvenile bad taste; repetitions and other lapses, accounts of minor visits, art criticism which he had outgrown or now thought banal, and many passages in which he had digressed excessively into 'phantastic visions' and 'flights of fancy'. And he cut out the first Letter in which he had stated his resolve to trace the internal adventures of his mind rather than the external encounters of his travels. ([19])

Few today would deny that the later book is better than the suppressed one; and all critics are agreed that the *Reminiscences of an Excursion to the Monasteries of Alcobaça and Batalha* his last work in this kind, is also the best, 'clear cool and lively in its tone, with just extravagance enough to give it colour and zest' (Oliver). Yet *Dreams, Waking Thoughts and Incidents* is a valuable document. In its fluent expression of a personality exploiting its sensibility to the full, it provides a striking example of Rousseauan romanticism. For the historian of literary psychology it is a proof of the power during the latter half of the eighteenth century of what may well be called 'Locke's Disease'—since it was John Locke who, in his *Essay on the Human Understanding,* first pointed out the dangers of unbridled mental Associations.

    King's College,
    University of London.

---

([19]) The two editions were collated by Hamish Miles in *The Travel-Diaries of William Beckford,* ed. G, Chapman, 1928, ii. Appendix.

# BECKFORD, PORTUGAL AND "CHILDISH ERROR"

### by
### MAGDI WAHBA

« ...*Le bonheur tient à l'énergie des principes ; il ne saurait y en avoir pour celui qui flotte sans cesse.* »

D. A. F. de Sade

There are few minor figures in English literary history who have engaged the attention of scholars and enthusiasts as much as William Beckford. I call him a minor figure advisedly, thus laying myself open to the scorn of those who are sealed of the tribe, with no implication of disrespect for the author of *Vathek* and of those Journals, which have been edited so expertly by Mr. Boyd Alexander. The case for Beckford's literary importance has been made only recently in an admirably comprehensive work by Dr. André Parreaux [1], whose wealth of documentation and ingenious eloquence would appear to confirm the earlier claims of Stéphane Mallarmé and Guy Chapman. It is, therefore, with the utmost diffidence that I venture to disagree with such distinguished Beckfordians and suggest that Beckford was a minor literary figure, but of the very first rank. One characteristic of major literary figures, which he lacked, was the concentration of the author's entire philosophic and aesthetic significance in his work, for it is almost impossible to consider Beckford's literary output divorced from the legend of "England's wealthiest son", the builder of Fonthill, the enthusiast for a Portugal which made him something of a national hero on the

---

[1] *William Beckford, auteur de 'Vathek' (1760-1844). Etude de la Création Littéraire.* (A.G. Nizet. Paris. 1960). pp. 75-6, 287-292, 387-397 and *Conclusion* passim.

very eve of its own collapse, the passionate homosexual, the sentimental widower and the agnostic with an inexplicable adoration for St. Anthony. His life was part of the very texture of his writings, and one cannot truly consider a major literary figure one who dispersed his genius in so many channels outside literature. This cannot be said of *Vathek,* however, which does stand on its own feet, as it were, an immoral or amoral oriental tale that is also very much more—an esoteric myth or perhaps an emblematic description of his own defiant singularity. This last interpretation which has been suggested by Dr. Parreaux ([2]) brings us back to the biographical interest in Beckford, an interest which perpetually draws our attention away from the actual work of art. This is sometimes true of other Romantics like Byron, Wordsworth or Shelley; our interest in their work is enhanced by what we know of their lives but we are first drawn to this biographical enquiry by a serious enjoyment of the actual work of literature. With Beckford, the work is a key to the personality, a record of a particularly acute and articulate sensibility and a companion to the 'legend'. If *Vathek* can be regarded as a sort of psychological allegory, the Journals are certainly in the direct line of descent from *The Sentimental Journey.*

There is a slight difference, however, for where Sterne viewed his travels through the prism of the self, almost neglecting the actual scenery on the way, Beckford lingered over every detail of the landscape, but absorbing it, as it were, into the landscape of his soul. He established correspondences between what he saw and what he felt, transforming the landscape into a setting for his sensibility, a symbolical representation of his melancholy and a pretext for irony. Incidents are not allowed to pass without their reminding him for instance, of the wife he has lost:

> *Saturday 29 September....* Mass was performed in my chapel this morning in honour of the valiant St. Michael. I assisted with apparent devotion, but could not help feeling

---

(2) *Ibid.* Chapter VII passim.

all the while more sympathy for the old Dragon than became a pious Catholic. Alas, we are both fallen angels! Six years ago how triumphantly did I pass this festival at Fonthill, seated at the foot of my father's statue, receiving the congratulations of the first personages in my nation, universally esteemed, looked up to and admired. The loss of Lady Margaret has harrowed up my feelings, or else the contrast between my present and past situation would have rushed this day into my mind with all its bitter circumstances, and almost driven me distracted; but I remained unmoved. I even dined with appetite and cheerfulness. (3)

Here the bitterness of his exile is opposed to the bitterness of remembering his loss of Lady Margaret and so irony is allowed to resolve the dilemma. But the memory of Lady Margaret haunts him after viewing a particularly beautiful landscape, or playing his own compositions on the piano, or watching fireworks in Marialva's palace (4). Reading Mrs. Frances Brooke's *The History of Lady Julia Mandeville*, his imagination "...took its flight to Fonthill, and pictured to itself the pale image of my Margaret." (5) Portugal was the setting for his mourning, a truly Romantic country of the heart, but it was also the place where Beckford, learning to forget the humiliations of England, could give free play to his natural high spirits and Voltairean sense of irony. It was this interplay between emotions, which were being recollected in an atmosphere of new excitements, and ironical detachment, that made it possible for him to observe the Portuguese landscape without the irritability and insularity of earlier British travellers. Beckford's Portugal was one which had greeted him so hospitably and had allowed him to live with its aristocracy on terms of such intimacy that he cannot have failed to realise the extraordinary opportunity which had been given to him to describe a country as no other British traveller had ever seen it.

---

(3) Boyd Alexander (ed.) *The Journal of William Beckford in Portugal and Spain, 1787-1788*. (London. 1954) pp. 213-214, cited hereafter as *Journal*.
(4) *Journal* pp. 62-63, 191, 234.
(5) *Ibid.* p. 227.

He availed himself of this opportunity in the Journal and recorded most of what he saw and much of what he felt and thought, but in *Italy ; with Sketches of Spain and Portugal* (⁶) he used his impressions to form a consciously artistic travel book, eliminating much that was personal or indiscreet. This sifting of his notes and careful editing produced a work which actually eclipsed his earlier *Vathek* for many critics. Commenting on it Oliver Elton went to the extent of writing :

> Beckford has a more accurate vision of foreign scenery than any English writer between Gray and Ruskin, Wordsworth not excluded. He revives the sleeping perception of colour, and finds the words for it (⁷).

His special gift lies in the description of landscapes which, it has been said, "invite immediate comparison with the landscapes of Claude Lorrain" (⁸) but what really lifts the work from being a collection of set pieces is Beckford's original concern with the pomp of ecclesiastical ceremonies and his awareness of the human element in his word pictures. Nothing in the part of the book dealing with Portugal excels his descriptions of crowds in church. The combination of Jomelli's sacred music, the bustle of worshippers whom he did not take quite seriously, the tolling of bells, and the extraordinary mixture of reverence and confusion which reigned on such occasions drew the best descriptions from his pen. Besides the church scenes his

---

(6) This work was published by Bentley in two volumes in July 1834. A second edition appeared in August of that year with the addition of a sonnet by Camoens (Letter XXX). There was an American edition which appeared in Philadelphia in the same year. There was also a Parisian edition in the same year bound up with *Vathek* and forming volume LIX of 'Baudry's Collection of Ancient and Modern Novels and Romances'. The third English edition appeared in 1835. (See André Parreaux: "Beckford et le Portugal" in *Bulletin des Etudes Portugaises*. Tomo xxxi. Lisbon 1958. pp. 8 and 54.)

(7) *A Survey of English Literature, 1780-1830* (London 1912) vol. I p. 208. *The Oxford Companion to English Literature* recommends this work (cited as a revised version of *Dreams, Waking Thoughts, and Incidents*) and *Recollections of an Excursion to the Monasteries of Alcobaça and Batalha* (1835) as giving more pleasure to the reader than *Vathek*.

(8) *Times Literary Supplement*. 2nd July 1954. p. 427.

descriptions of the noisy hubbub of town life in Portugal, the tragi-comic grotesqueness of the poverty and the picturesqueness of life in the streets of Lisbon are the best. He was happiest in the description of crowds from which he could remain aloof as though he were looking at a sort of southern Breughel, for the solitary and Romantic figures in the 'Lorrain' landscapes were all rather narcissistic representations of Beckford himself, whose graceful melancholy could become cloying.

It is interesting that Portugal elicited what was best in Beckford's descriptive genius. Once he had gone to Spain the crowds, the churches and the teeming streets were ignored, while Beckford's own sentimental life seems to have occupied his pen. The charms of Mohammed and of the equally seductive young Prince and Princesse de Listenais engaged his attention throughout the Spanish part of his Journal. One might venture to suggest that Portugal was the scene of his most important psychological experiences and that his first Portuguese journey helped him to decide on the true nature of his tastes and to fix the main features of his personality to his own satisfaction and for the rest of his life. The splendid reception, the opportunities of settling in Portugal, marrying and perhaps being made a grandee, all this was just the right therapy for the humiliation of his loss of character in England. A new dimension was added to his personality for he was able to rise above the image of himself as the defiant yet sensitive victim of calumny, the reprobate of the Powderham scandal and the rich man who had been refused a peerage. He was able to think of these setbacks in their right perspective. England was not the world ; reputations are not lost irretrievably if one has the means to enter into new associations, to travel like a prince and to shed the inhibitions of a Protestant upbringing. Portugal, much more than Switzerland, had helped him to accede to that cosmopolitanism which was the mark of the eighteenth century gentleman, who could rise above the petty restrictions of class and nation. [9]

---

(9) See review of *Beckford* by Guy Chapman (London. 1937) in *Times Literary Supplement* 13th March 1937.

Being under no obligation to frequent the English Factory, he was able to throw himself into Portuguese aristocratic life without reservations. Had he consented to become naturalised, however, and to change his official religion, he would have lost the freedom of cosmopolitanism and exchanged the constrictions of English life for those of a much more wooden Portuguese society. It was essential for Beckford's new-found peace of mind that he should not belong to either country in any sense which would cramp his freedom of action. Having been judged once he had to ensure enough mobility to escape further judgement, and Portugal would eventually prove as merciless as England, if he gave her a chance. Meanwhile, he was being fêted and loved and it was probably a sort of extravagant gratitude which encouraged him to indulge in that half-serious cult of St. Anthony of Padua (a saint born in Portugal and almost idolised in Lisbon).

In Portugal he learned to accept another fact about himself: that he was what Mrs. Thrale called "a Professor of Paederasty" ([10]). From 1779 to 1788 Beckford's sexual tastes appear to have been ambivalent. "The dogs spared me and it was tolerably cool", he wrote towards the beginning of his Portuguese Journal, "so I am better this morning and should like another race with the Irish girl or the *meninos* at the Patriarchal, whichever would most please Providence. I am resigned to whatever I meet with." ([11]) Yet there is little doubt that he really preferred boys. "Les sentiments qu'il a éprouvés pour Louisa", writes Dr. Parreaux "sont loin d'avoir eu l'intensité de ceux qu'il éprouvait dans le même temps pour William Courtenay. En fait, Louisa ne semble avoir réussi à se faire accepter comme maîtresse de Beckford qu'en se subordonnant d'elle-même à Courtenay, peut-être même en servant d'intermédiaire, en tous cas en favorisant la liaison des deux jeunes gens". ([12])

---

(10) Katherine Balderston (ed.) *Thraliana* (Oxford 1942), vol. II p. 969, note.

(11) *Journal*, pp. 56-57.

(12) Parreaux: *op cit.*, p. 56.

There is no doubt, furthermore, that Dom Pedro was loved with much more warmth than poor Madame de Santa Cruz and that the Princesse de Listenais was only a means for a more piquant relationship with her husband, as the Portuguese and Spanish Journals show so clearly. When the Marchioness of Marialva asked him to watch over a favourite nephew of hers being educated in Paris, he confided to his Journal: "Rare sport, thought I" (13). After Portugal and after a brief episode in Spain his sexual tastes appear to have become exclusively paederastic. The death of his wife, his loss of character in England and the implied forgiveness of his welcome in Portugal made him feel free to shed the mask. "How tired I am of keeping a mask on my countenance. How tight it sticks—it makes me sore. There's metaphor for you. I have all the fancies and levity of a child and would give an estate or two to skip about the galleries of the Patriarchal with the *menino* unobserved." (14) If he did not always enjoy this freedom in Portugal itself, where it would have been ungrateful to abuse Marialva's splendid hospitality, he certainly lived under no similar restraint in Spain or in England after his return. "Barzaba", the name he assumed in his letters to Franchi, when he was in pursuit of boys, would have had no scruples about turning Fonthill into a homosexual paradise, but it appears that Franchi was not always successful in pandering to his tastes.

Paederasty was not uncommon among Beckford's contemporaries; it was practised as a sort of voluptuous refinement by men who would certainly not have regarded themselves as sodomites. Casanova himself had not disdained such pleasures and the reputation for such practices floated around the names of M.G. Lewis, Richard Heber, William Combe, the Marquis of Townshend, and the Bishop of Clogher, who was arrested with a young Guardsman in the *White Lion,* St. James's in 1822. Having lost his character once Beckford was very discreet about indulging his inclinations. These inclinations were not, however, the

---

(13) *Journal,* p. 273.
(14) *Ibid.* p. 41.

extreme refinements of a voluptuary, or even the more common, and pathological type of inversion. They were part of a general obsession with 'childishness' which pervades most of Beckford's personal reveries.

Dr. Parreaux has recently pointed out the importance of this 'childishness' for an understanding of Beckford's psychological make-up :

> Il est manifeste que notre héros éprouve *un sentiment érotique violent pour sa propre image d'enfant* et qu'il s'efforce de la retrouver chez Courtenay, D. Pedro, etc. Il essaye, en quelque sorte, de l'objectiver en nouant des rapports étroits avec de jeunes garçons : *l'homosexualité, chez Beckford, est au fond une forme de narcissisme* ([15])

Beckford's narcissistic paederasty would explain the frequent references to childishness in his correspondence and his description of himself in his Journal as a 'poor childish animal' ([16]) or as a person 'still retaining the appearance, the agility and the fancy of a stripling' ([17]). Such references are significant, but so are the various associations of all the experiences which he finds most pleasing and beautiful with 'childishness'. "I cannot help flattering myself", he writes in his Journal

> that my compositions resembled those of my dear Lady Hamilton, those pastoral movements full of childish bewitching melody I have heard her so frequently compose during the autumn I passed at Caserta. ([18])

The freshness and innocence of childhood were the twin elements of beauty for him, of beauty in what was outside himself and of the beauty which he felt was part of himself. When he was only twenty he had written to Alexander Cozens : "How firmly am I resolved to be a Child for ever !" ([19])

---

(15) Parreaux: *op. cit.*, p. 68.
(16) *Journal*, pp. 49 and 124.
(17) *Ibid.*, p. 224.
(18) *Ibid.*, p. 191.
(19) Lewis Melville: *The Life and Letters of William Beckford of Fonthill...* (London 1910) p. 96.

## BECKFORD, PORTUGAL AND "CHILDISH ERROR"

A very complex psychological image of 'childishness' can be gathered from all these statements: First, it was one of the constituent elements of pleasing and beautiful experiences, it was the secret key to a sensibility which shrunk from adult experience and yearned for a pastoral paradise of innocent joys. This was different from the Wordsworthian nostalgia for the visionary world of childhood and not quite the same as the Proustian recreation of a world which had disappeared with his childhood for, artificially and by an effort of the will, Beckford clung to the sensibility of his childhood throughout his life. Secondly, it was a sign of what Dr. Parreaux recognizes as narcissism but a narcissism tinged with masochism: the *alter ego* of the Beckford-Peter Pan image must become a prey to Barzaba, the monstrous voluptuary who is ever panting for new victims. Louisa, using every subterfuge to hold Beckford, was to recognise this need when she wrote, offering her own son, aged four:

> I am miserable now I have a little victim in training to sacrifice on your altar. I wish to God my William was old enough for it. He grows every day more and more beautiful, and will in a few years answer your purpose to perfection... [20]

The figure of Beckford as a self-devouring child wishing to rape his own image in all his paederastic adventures is only one of the possible explanations for what has been called 'Beckfordian Satanism' [21]. The Satanism of his Romantic contemporaries was a principle of cruel energy seeking to leave an indelible mark on the world and so conquer death and oblivion. With Beckford Satanism was a sort of game, perhaps only a verbal game, an attempt to show off and to mystify. The Satanic references in his correspondence with Louisa suggest, wrote Guy Chapman, "that both Beckford and Louisa were indulging themselves in black magic, perhaps what is known as the Black

---

[20] Quoted from the Hamilton Papers in Guy Chapman: *Beckford* (London 1937) p. 117.
[21] Parreaux: *op. cit.* p. 372.

Mass, a species of mummery which sometimes appeals to the imaginative adolescent". (22)

The third possible interpretation of Beckford's 'childishness' is the obvious one that being a child implied that one was not held responsible for one's actions. Psychologically, it meant that Beckford felt himself free to indulge in the preservation of a childish dream world dominated by a supremely beautiful and gifted Child, who combined the tragic and ruthless irresponsibility of Vathek and Nouronihar with the humble and happy irresponsibility of Gulchenrouz. This Child, though rich and well connected, was outside the accepted English class system, bored by Parliament but yearning for a peerage as for a glittering bauble. A Child could not lose character for it could only be guilty of "childish error", which deserved a scolding at the utmost and then called for the sunshine of forgiveness. England, however, was not prepared to see Beckford in this light: moneyed vulgarian though he might be, a peerage was not beyond his grasp, but he would have to deserve it, either by taking some interest in Parliament or, at least, avoiding scandal. After his retirement to Fonthill and then to Bath, when he carefully doctored his notes and correspondence in order to redeem his reputation, it was too late because England had progressed even further towards the ideals of nineteenth century respectability.

Beckford's private world of 'childishness' was not simply a form of human singularity which found its expression in his writings. He chose to live in what Dr. Parreaux has called "un monde imaginaire réel" (23), like Byron, Gérard de Nerval and Ludwig II of Bavaria, whose attempts ended in early death or insanity, but Beckford's wealth and longevity allowed him to prolong the dream beyond the bounds of a mere splendid protest.

What, it may not be too idle to ask oneself, would Beckford have written if he had not been "England's wealthiest son"? There is no doubt that most of his writings about his travels

---

(22) Guy Chapman: *op. cit.* p. 102.
(23) Parreaux: *op. cit.* p. 75.

would have lost much of their piquancy, but had he been able to travel at all, he would certainly have described the foreign crowds he was so gifted at representing in all their picturesqueness and squalor. There might have been less of St. Anthony, perhaps less of the ecstatic writing about singing and instrumental music, but the grandeur of Jomelli's church music would have been recaptured, the landscapes with the minute attention to botanical detail (a characteristic English traveller's interest) would have remained, and also the ironical yet not malicious renderings of his encounters with people in the streets of a foreign city. His *Recollections of an Excursion to the Monasteries of Alcobaça and Batalha* would not have seen the light and this would have been a very great pity, as even non-Beckfordians will concede. *Vathek* would certainly have been written, but probably in English, and many of his unpublished Oriental Tales would have found their way to some literary periodical. That he would have been a writer there is little doubt because his passion for writing was certainly genuine enough. "He was, in fact," wrote Guy Chapman, "abominably industrious. Over *Dreams, Waking Thoughts and Incidents* he spent months. After the first hot fit, he laboured for years upon *Vathek* and the *Episodes*. He never hesitated to try to better each edition of his books." ([24]) It is unlikely, however, that he would have belonged to any Grub Street coterie or that he would have done any hack work. He had little patience for the writers of his age: *Modern Novel Writing* was a withering satire on the lady novelists (who included his own half-sister, Mrs. Hervey); he was not impressed by Dr. Johnson and found Boswell's *Life* extremely tedious: "Never were two heavy folios closer suffered with German arbitrary maxims, trifling anecdotes, mad digressions and idle chit-chat" ([25]) and he detested Gibbon with a sort of passion. After his retirement he read voraciously but was full of contempt for Coleridge, Shelley and, rather

---

(24) Guy Chapman: *op. cit.* p. 191.
(25) Quoted from the Hamilton Papers in J.W. Oliver: *The Life of William Beckford* (London 1932) p. 210.

ungratefully, Byron. He was bored by Scott and by Samuel Rogers, but later his enthusiasm rallied for the early novels of Benjamin Disraeli, and then even they began to pall. Only Beckford was suitable reading for Beckford.

A poorer Beckford would still have been a writer and perhaps necessity would have made him *write* his Romantic revolt instead of just *living* it. An indifferent poet, he would hardly have been able to compete with the great poets of the Romantic Revival. On the other hand, his temper was too capricious to make him a good critic. He might have excelled as a Gothic novelist with his tongue in his cheek, but not for long. He would still be remembered as the author of *Vathek* and of some conjectural, yet certainly delightful, travel books.

With all his gifts, Beckford did not have the singleness of purpose, the fanaticism, which go into the making of literary greatness. Outside literature he dispersed these gifts and did not allow himself to become sufficiently engrossed in one of his many activities. Vathek and Gulchenrouz tore at his soul, which remained divided to the end of his long life, unhappy, sterile, lonely and, finally, unloved.

# BECKFORD, *VATHEK* and THE ORIENTAL TALE*

*by*

## FATMA MOUSSA MAHMOUD

*Vathek,* is no unique performance, but an epitome of most of the leading characteristics of 'the Oriental tale as already developed in the East and copied and modified in Europe, (Stanley Lane-Poole "The Author of *Vathek*", *Quaterly Review* (October 1910), p. 382.)

When Galland published the first volumes of his translation of the curious tales he had acquired in Aleppo, French readers were fascinated by the charming sultana weaving tales to save her head, even for a Thousand and One Nights. (¹) Soon their English neighbours (²) were to fall under the spell of the neverending tales. Those who might be expected to look down on such a frivolous pastime were assured that:

> ....All Orientals, Persians, Tartars and Indians, there appear just as they are, from sovereigns down to people of the lowest condition. Thus the reader will have the pleasure of seeing them act and hearing them speak without taking the trouble of travelling to seek them in their countries. (³).

---

(*) Based on Chapters VII and VIII of *The Oriental Tale in England in the Early Nineteenth Century, 1786-1824,* Ph. D. Thesis, University of London, 1957.

(1) Antoine Galand (1646-1715) was one of the French sovereign's 'Jeunes de Langues', who served in the Near East for some years as secretary of the French Embassy in Constantinople. His translation was first published in 1704. For a detailed study, see — Conant, Martha Pike. *The Oriental Tale in England in the Eighteenth Century,* New York, Columbia University Press, 1908. & Martino, Pierre. *L'Orient dans la littérature Française au XVIIe et XVIIIe siècles,* Paris, 1906.

(2) The date of the first English edition is not known but a *fourth* edition was published for Andrew Bell, London, 1713. For details see Conant *op. cit.*

((3) Advertisement to Galland's translation of the *Arabian Nights.*

To counter-act the scoffings of the more determined stalwarts of 'good taste', that the tales were no more than a French forgery, editors of some English translations quoted travellers' accounts testifying to the authenticity of the manners depicted in the strange book. (4)

The eccentric Edward Wortley Montagu acquired a complete manuscript of the original exotic work, which passing through the hands of one man of letters after another, was finally placed at the Bodleian Library. (5)

In France the instant favour with which the tales were met, encouraged another Jeune de Langues, Petis de la Croix to publish the *Turkish Tales* (1707) and follow them with *Persian Tales, or a Thousand and One Days* (1710-1712). Soon preposterous imitations of every kind were to follow. The pseudo translations by T. Simon Gueulette of *Chinese Tales, Mogul Tales, Tartarian Tales* and *Peruvian Tales* are examples of the best known of these imitations. English translations were issued in Britain almost as soon as copies arrived from the continent.

The majority of these imitations pretended to a similar origin as the *Arabian Nights,* but in most cases the alleged translators were not as ready to produce the original manuscript.

In the preface to the French 'translation' (6) of the *Persian*

---

(4) Lady Mary Wortley Montagu's *Letters from Turkey* (1716-18) were quoted by the Rev. Edward Forster, editor of one of the "elegant" editions of the *Arabian Nights,* 1802. Another traveller often brought forward for the same purpose was James Capper whose *Observations on the Passage to India through Egypt,* (London, 1783) testified that the *Arabian Nights* were "in the same estimation all over Asia, that the adventures of Don Quixote are in Spain...", E. Forester's edition of the *Nights* (London, 1802) vol. I, p. XLIII.

(5) This MS of the *Arabian Nights* was the copy used by W. Beckford. It was apparently the property of the Duke of Bedford. It was sold in 1787 to Dr. Joseph White, professor of Hebrew and Arabic at Oxford, from whom it passed to Jonathan Scott, who finally sold it to the Bodleian Library for £ 50 in 1803. See R.F. Burton's Introduction to *Supplemental Nights,* vol. VI, 1888.

(6) Petis de la Croix was long accused of having invented these tales. For the rehabilitation of the fame of this long disgraced orientalist see, Victor Chauvin, *Bibilographie des Ouvrages Arabes ou relatifs aux Arabes, publiés dans l'Europe Chrétienne de 1810 à 1885,* Liège, 1892... vol. IV, pp. 124-5.

*Tales,* Petis de la Croix gave his accoount of the origin of the tales as follows :

> Nous devons ces contes .... au célèbre Dervis Moclès, que la Perse met au nombre de ses grands personnages. Il était chef des sopis d'Ispahan et il avait douze disciples .... Moclès étant fort jeune s'avisa de traduire en persan des comédies indiennes, qui ont été traduites en toutes les langues orientales, et dont on voit à la bibliothèque du roi une traduction turque sous le titre de *Alfarage Baad Alschida* .... Mais le traducteur persan, pour donner à son ouvrage un air original, mit ces comédies en contes, qu'il appela Hesaryek-Rouz, c'est-à-dire Mille-et-un jours. Il confia son manuscrit au sieur Petis de la Croix, qui était en liaison d'amitié avec lui à Ispahan en 1675, et même il lui permit d'en prendre une copie. (7)

Throughout the eighteenth century contributors to the oriental tale conformed to two main features of this new *genre* : the frame tale including so many tales within a tale, and the device of the oriental man of letters who presents the European traveller with a manuscript of tales (later developed into an account of his adventures). (8) All composed learned introductions evoking the phantoms of one 'Dervis Moclès' or another, to keep up the fiction of their alleged translations. (9)

The first half of the eighteenth century saw a profusion of such translations copied from the French, and soon many English writers also learned "to turn a Persian tale for half a crown".

With the establishment of the English East India Company as a more or less supreme authority in India in the sixties, (10) another class of contributors to the 'oriental tale' began to appear

---

(7) *Ibid,* pp. 123-4, n. 2.

(8) J.J. Morier pretended that the manuscript of *Hajji Baba* (1824) was entrusted to him by the hero—an old acquaintance—at a chance meeting in the Levant. Thomas Hope did the same in *Anastasius* (1818).

(9) For an interesting satire on this device see Horace Walpole's *Hieroglyphic Tales* (Strawebery Hill, 1785). The preface is a clever parody of the pretentious and would be scholarly prefaces to oriental tales.

(10) By 1761 the English had beaten their French and Dutch rivals in India. The terms of the Peace of Paris, 1763 recognized the supremacy of the English in that sphere and France was virtually evicted from India.

on the scene; servants of the Company began to add their own contribution to the fashionable literary *genre*. In 1764, the Rev James Ridley, Chaplain to the East India Company, published the *Tales of the Genii*, (11) pretending they were a translation from a 'Persian Manuscript', by Sir Charles Morell, a traveller. At the end of the *Tales*, however, the Reverend gentleman gave up the pretence of Sir C. Morell and admitted that the Genii were fled. They had been there only to illustrate a moral tale to Christian readers.

Direct, authentic translations were to follow, but slowly and haltingly at first. In 1768, Alexander Dow, a former officer in the army of the East India Company published two small volumes of tales that came to be known as the *Tales of Inatulla*. (12) The phantom figure of the 'Dervish Moclès' assumed the more tangible shape of the 'Persian Munshee' or scribe, who in the course of instructing the servant of the Company in the intricacies of Persian (the language of letters, commerce and diplomacy in India), put the manuscript of the Tales in his hands, to exercise his newly acquired capacity for translation. Like the *Persian Tales* of Petis de la Croix they were attributed to an Indian origin. The English translator apologised for the occasional licentiousness of the *Tales*, and admitted that he had not chosen them for any particular merit; it was merely by accident that he had translated them as an exercise in the Persian language.

In spite of Dow's misgivings about their reception the *Tales of Inatulla* seem to have been well received at their publication, as the *Oriental Collections* asserted in 1797 that the public had bought up the edition "with avidity". A French translation was also sold out. (13)

---

(11) *Tales of the Genii: or... Delightful Lessons of Horam, the Son of Asmar...* tr. from the Persian Manuscript by Sir C. Morell, 2 vols., 1764. Other editions were issued 1780, 1785, 1794 and the tales were included in Weber's *Tales of the East* (Edinburgh, 1812), III, 417-589.

(12) Inayat-Allah, *Tales. Translated from the Persian of Inatulla of Delhi*. (By A. Dow), 2 vols., London, 1768.

(13) See Sir William Ouseley's *Oriental Collections* (1797), 288-9.

Was that the beginning of the counter-current across the Channel of direct authentic translations, which characterised the oriental tale of the nineteenth century? It was early yet: Colonel Dow in 1768 was rather a solitary figure and even his work was thirty years later pronounced to have been "an imitation rather than translation". (14) The soldier-trader servants of the East India Company were still the hardy adventurers fighting behind Clive or the young Hastings in the political chaos of India in mid-eighteenth century. The spark of cultural pre-occupation which Sir William Jones was to kindle in Calcutta in the Eighties was yet to come.

In England the book-sellers still depended on France for fashionable 'oriental tales'. English writers still used the aerial undefined background of the East to point a moral or adorn a tale. The mood was changing to rather a mocking supercilious tone with the translation of French parodies of the extravagant oriental tales, but the alleged Oriental, the original writer of the tale still figured in the Preface. He sometimes even made his appearance as a wise Chinese or an innocent Persian, for some time resident in London or Paris, whose 'correspondence' or innocent 'impressions' would for some reason fall into the hands of a Goldsmith or any impoverished man of letters living by his wits to be 'translated' to their English readers. But more commonly still, he was the fabulous Oriental who entrusted his manuscript of the tale or tales to a traveller, who might or might not be the translator himself.

---

(14) *loc cit.* In 1790 Jonathan Scott published a more literal translation of the same tales as the *Bahar Danush* or, *Garden of Knowledge, An Oriental Romance* : Translated from the *Persic of Einaint Oollah...*, 3. vols., Shrewsberry. 1790. In the preface he savagely criticised Dow's version. As a further proof of the faithfulness of *his* version, he announced that the Persian text would be placed in the British Museum for the inspection of any-one competent to do so.

FATMA MOUSSA MAHMOUD

## AN ARABIAN TALE, FROM AN UNPUBLISHED MANUSCRIPT (1786) :-

The *Morning Chronicle* of June 7th, 1786 carried an advertisement, running:

Caliph Vathek
This Day is published in small 8 vo. Price 4s.

*The History of the Caliph Vathek*
*An Arabian Tale from an unpublished Manuscript*
with Notes Critical and Explanatory
Printed for J. Johnson, No. 72, St. Paul's Churchyard
A few copies, on large paper, price 7/6 in boards :

For all an outside observer could see, the book that appeared under this title could be one of the host of such *Tales* translated from 'unpublished manuscripts'. There were not many among the readers of 1786 who could give any authoritive opinion on the subject. The editor stated in his Preface :

> The Original of the following story, with some others of a similar kind, collected in the East by a Man of letters, was communicated to the Editor above three years ago. The pleasure he received from the perusal of it, induced him at that time to transcribe and since to translate it.

He went on to speak of,

> ....the difficulty of accommodating our English idioms to the Arabick, preserving the correspondent tones of a diversified narration, and discriminating the nicer touches of character through the shades of foreign manners... [15]

Readers turning to the story itself could easily believe the editor. The opening, reminiscent of *Johnson's Rasselas* (1759), at once introduced a real Caliph of the Abassides. Though the Caliph was not Haroun el-Rashid whose name had become so familiar to readers of the *Arabian Nights,* he was one of his successors, and the curious could check up his authenticity in D'Herbelot's *Bibliothèque Orientale,* to which the notes promptly referred them.

---

[15] *An Arabian Tale, from An Unpublished Manuscript;* with Notes. London, J. Johnson, 1786, p. 111.

There were also reminiscences of the *Persian Tales*. The Caliph had rather a strange quality: when he was angry, one of his eyes became so terrible that anyone upon whom it was fixed fell back instantly, sometimes dead.

> For fear, however, of depopulating his dominions and making his palace desolate, he but rarely gave way to his anger. (16)

The heroine of the *Persian Tales* was so beautiful that people thronged round to gaze at her, in spite of the guards who beat them off, often killing some of the most timorous.

> The King nearly touched with the calamities which the charms of his daughter drew upon his subjects, resolved to withdraw her from the eyes of men : he laid his commands upon her never to go out of the palace ; so that the people saw her no more (17)

Like the heroine of the *Persian Tales*, Nouronihar, the heroine of *Vathek* had a nurse who strangely enough was also called Sutlememe. The Sutlememe of *Vathek* like her namesake of the *Persian Tales*, was taken in confidence by the heroine's father and attempted to extract him for a predicament in which his strong-willed daughter, had placed him.

The *History of the Caliph Vathek*, contained the stock themes common to oriental tales previously published, love, adventure, magic and the quest for hidden treasure. The Caliph Vathek dominated by an unquenchable thirst for knowledge forbidden to man, built himself a tower where he and his mother Carathis, a most fiendish woman, practised magic, observed stars and in general led a most impious life. Vathek was once visited by a strange creature from far off lands. The Giaour, as the stranger is called throughout the book, seduced the Caliph with strange treasures and showed such mysterious powers that Vathek, egged on by his mother the sorceress Carathis, signed a Faustian pact with the horrid creature. He offered him the life of some fifty innocent boys, children of his most faithful cour-

---

(16) *Ibid.*, 1 - 2.
(17) Weber, Henry. *Tales of the East* (1812), II, 307.

tiers, in exchange for the key of the subterranean palace where the talismans and treasures of the pre-Adamite kings and of Soliman-Ben-Daoud were deposited.

Having performed this libation to appease the Giaour whom he had angered, the Caliph proceeded on his quest to the ruins of ancient Istakhar (Persepolis), where the Portal of Ebony was to open and admit him. The Caliph set out in a most sumptuous cavalcade, accompanied by his wives, eunuchs and servants of every kind. He left his wicked mother to administer to the government of his dominions with the help of his vizier, the good Morakanabad. Half way on his long journey "to sit on the throne of Soliman" the Caliph's wonderful cavalcade was attacked by storms and wild beasts. The whole party was threatened with destruction, when emissaries of a pious Emir arrived to invite the Caliph to the seat of their good master. Though Vathek violated the injunctions of *his* master by entering the abode of such a good man, he made up for his own disobedience by seducing the Emir's daughter Nouronihar. Here we are introduced to a feminine character powerfully and most originally conceived. The young fawn-like daughter of the Emir Fakreddin was betrothed to her cousin Gulchenrouz, a stripling of her own age who still lingered with her in the harem instead of starting his manly training in the field. The two were extremely fond of each other, singing verses and playing music together, and listening to tales told by the old nurse Sutlememe. But the young girl soon shot ahead of her companion. At the touch of the superior and more masculine Caliph, she matured into a woman of hitherto unsuspected qualities. The wicked and ambitious Caliph made her as heartless and as selfish as himself. The Emir in his despair conspired with the old nurse and Shaban the old tutor to drug his daughter and nephew with a narcotic powder that would give them the appearance of death. They would be secretely conveyed to a secret place in the valley until the evil Caliph had departed. To dissuade Nouronihar from seeking him, Sutlememe and Shaban would pretend that they had killed themselves in despair. The two pious, sermon-preaching dwarfs would add to the 'local colour' of a place after death where the heroine and her cousin were to be corrected of the little faults of their love. The plan proceeded in due course, but the Caliph instead of departing on his quest, lingered at the place where his beloved was supposed to be buried. Like the Megnoun of the Arabian romance, he raved emaciated with hunger and watching and would not quit the spot of his Leila's grave. Finally he and Nouronihar met and discovered the Emir's device. She was henceforth his favourite and only wife. She soon vied with the Caliph in irreverence and even showed more courage than her mate when confronted by the sight of Eblis himself.

To atone for his delay in presenting himself at the Palace of Subterranean Fire, Vathek committed as many sacrileges on his way to Istakar, as lay in his power. On reaching the valley of Rocnabad (made famous by Sir William Jones's translation of Hafiz), he ordered his men to level down all the oratories and sanctuaries with which the famous valley abounded. The Santons and Sheikhs, he punished and disgraced to the delight of his beloved Nouronihar, who was now hardened up in the pursuit of the Carbuncle of Giamschid and the throne of Soliman.

When the Caliph finally arrived at the end of his quest, the ruins of Istakar discovered a steep staircase and the Giaour waiting at the bottom with the golden key of the portal of ebony, that was to admit the culprits to their heart's desire. Vathek and Nouronihar found themselves in the domains of Eblis, who sat on his throne, a globe of fire, on a lofty eminence under a tabernacle hung around with the skins of leopards. The Prince of Rebels received the homage of his newly recruited subjects and courteously invited them to enjoy all the treasures and talismans that his dominions could offer to gratify their insatiable curiosity. They soon discovered, however, that in achieving their wish, they had also condemned themselves to the worst of all possible punishments. Though they could command the Afrits and Jinn to admit them to the most hidden of secret treasures and to the awful presence of Soliman-Ben-Daoud himself, the sight of the once powerful monarch, with his heart enveloped in flames, gave them an insight into what awaited them. They, like the multitude that inhabited the subterranean regions of Eblis, were to lose "the most precious gift of heaven

— HOPE". They were to wander aimlessly in those regions of gloom, their hearts on fire, showing through the crystal transparence of their chests, the right hand to their hearts, and their eyes expressing nothing but hatred and abhorrence for one another.

The tale which started in a tone of supercilious lighthearted mocking ended on a note of awful tragedy, as if the reader too were to realise with the damned Caliph, the result of his previous indulgence :

> Thus the Caliph Vathek, who, for the sake of empty pomp and forbidden power, had sullied himself with a thousand crimes, became a prey to grief without end, and remorse without mitigation ; whilst the humble, the despised Gulchenrouz passed whole ages in undisturbed tranquillity, and in the pure happiness of childhood. (18).

The catastrophe was more tragic than anything reported in the oriental tales translated so far. It was more in the character of Dante's *Inferno* than the adventures of treasure seeking oriental heroes. The character of Eblis recalled Milton's Satan rather than the mischievous perverse character of the fallen angel depicted in the Koran to which Moslem imagination of the Devil strictly conforms. There is nothing noble or awe inspiring in the figure of Eblis as pictured by Moslem imagination, but the sovereign at whose throne Vathek and Nouronihar paid their respects was different. Seated on the globe of fire that made his throne and surrounded by

> an infinity of elders with streaming beards, and afrits in complete armour... ...His person was that of a young man, whose noble and regular features seemed to have been tarnished by malignant vapours. In his large eyes appeared both pride and despair [the stock emotions that were to rule the Satanic hero], his flowing hair retained some semblance to that of an angel of light. In his hand, which thunder had blasted, he swayed the iron sceptre, that causes the monster Ouranabad, the afrits and all the powers of the abyss to tremble (19)

---

(18) *An Arabian Tale... op. cit.*, 211.
(19) *Ibid.*, 194.

Nouronihar was certainly surprised at the encounter,

> ...she could not help admiring the person of Eblis for, she expected to have seen some stupendous giant.

He ironically enough, addressed the culprits as "Creatures of clay", but his voice had attributes that could only be the product of a late eighteenth century imagination. It was,

> ...more mild than might be imagined, but such as penetrated the soul and filled it with the deepest melancholy. [20]

He played the perfect host and invited his new subjects to enjoy all the pleasures afforded by his domains. When their doom was sealed and their punishment announced, it was not he who did the nasty job, but an unidentified voice thundered the sentence from above. With the impetuous insolent Carathis, he showed most gentlemanly self-control and preserved his dignity by disappearing in the curtains of his tabernacle.

The catastrophe was not pure Milton and Dante; important details were borrowed from previously published pseudo-oriental tales. The incident of the flaming hearts was borrowed from Gueullette's *Mogul Tales,* though the author of *Vathek* had clearly improved upon the original. The sufferers in the *Mogul Tales,*

> ... unbottoned their waistcoats and through their skin, which appeared like crystal, ...their hearts compassed with fire, by which, though burnt without ceasing, yet they were ...never consumed [21].

Another such spurious oriental tale, also translated from the French, had supplied the original image of Eblis sitting on the glofe of fire, the Faustian pact with the agent of the Devil and part of the machinery of *Vathek*. In one of the episodes of *The Adventures of Abdalla son of Hanif* (Paris, 1712 tr. into English,

---

(20) *Ibid.,* 195.
(21) Quoted by Conant, M.P. *op. cit.,* p. 36.

1729) (²²), Prince Dilsenguin had been seduced by a subject of Eblis, in the same manner as Vathek.

Nothing can better illustrate the importance of *Vathek* (1786) as a land-mark between the eighteenth century oriental tale and the ninettenth century type, than comparing it with *Abadalla Son of Hanif*. Though the influence of the earlier book is clear in *Vathek*, there is no further similarity. The former was one of the most insipid of oriental tales produced by the eighteenth century. No one who looked at the frontspiece of the Paris edition of 1712 could doubt for a moment that the book was a gross imitation. The ridiculous youth, apparently the hero Abdalla, dressed faultlessly as an eighteenth century gentleman of fashion, with wig, long buttoned coat, breeches and stockings, watch and chain, etc... is highly in contrast with the perfect 'costume' of *Vathek* (to use Byron's apt word). Though a reader well-read in both oriental tales and European literature might have suspected from the above, particularly from the descent into Hell that the author of *Vathek* could have been none but a European, this was offset by the great care paid to details of local colour. Such care might well have deceived readers brought up on spurious glaring imitations of oriental tales.

The names as mentioned above were reminiscent of the *Arabian Nights* and the *Persian Tales*. (²³) The Caliph himself was a real historical figure, though his name should have been properly written, Al-Wathek Billah. D'Herbelot's version of Vathek was near enough and he was truly the son of Motassem. When a rebellion broke out, it was headed by his brother

---

(22) *Les Aventures d'Abdalla fils d'Hanif..., Traduites en français sur le manuscrit arabe trouvé à Batavia par M de Sandisson,* Paris 1712, was really composed in French by Jean Paul Bignon. There were four other French editions, 1713, 1723 (2 ed.), 1773. It was included in the *Bibliothèque Universelle des Romans,* January 1778. The English translation by William Hatchett (1729), was also included in Weber's *Tales of the East* (1812), III, 591-736.

(23) One of the Vathek's wives is called Dilara cf. the story of "Coloufe and Dilara" in *The Persian Tales*. Nouronihar (Light of Day) is the name of a hreoine in the *Arabian Nights*, with whom four brothers fall in love at the same time.

Motavakel (Al-Motuakkel Billah), and though there was no such rebellion in record, European readers of 1786 were not very conversant with the particulars of the history of the Abbassides. His capital was truly Samarah built some leagues outside Bagdad to house the Caliph's growing household. It was not just the aerial Bagdat, Grand Cairo or Babylon on the Nile of other oriental tales.

## THE ITINERARY :-

The quest of the irreverent Caliph lay in the ruins of the alleged temples of the Sun in the ancient Persepolis or Istakhar which according to Richardson ([24]) meant the temple, the dwelling or the praise of the sun. His itinerary was rather undefined at first, but after the rescue by Emir Fakherdin, it was well mapped. It followed closely the route of seventeenth and early eighteenth century travellers who had travelled the same way. The valley of the Emir was presumably not far from Schiraz where Bababalouk sent for fragrant wine. Four days after Vathek had finally left the valley of his unhappy host behind, he arrived at Rochnabad, where he received the deputies from Schiraz whom he most viciously disgraced. On leaving Rocnabad the route was most definitely delineated :

> ...the expedition proceeded ; leaving Schiraz on the right, and verging towards a large plain ; from whence were discernible, on the edge of the horizon, the dark summits of the mountains of Istakar ([25])

There the Caliph suffered his last chance of salvation to escape and scorned the messenger of Heaven who presented himself to the now doomed hero in the guise of a shepherd ([26]). The

---

(24) Richardson, John. *Dissertation on the Languages, Literature, and Manners of Eastern Nations* (Oxford, 1777), was for more than forty years one of the main sources of information on the East used by English writers.

(25) *An Arabian Tale...* (1786), 180.

(26) For a detailed comparison with Marlowe's *Dr. Faustus* and Addison's *Vision of Mirza*, see May, Marcel. *La Jeunesse de William Beckford et la génèse de son 'Vathek'*, Paris Les Presses Universitaires de France, 1928, pp. 264-5.

Caliph's unholy ambition was fired by Nouronihar's impatience to sit on the throne of Soliman's consort Balkis (the Queen of Sheba) and command the powers of darkness :

> ...they advanced by moon-light, till they came within view of the two towering rocks that form a kind of portal to the valley, at the extremity of which, rose the vast ruins of Istakar. Aloft, on the mountain, glimmered the fronts of various royal mausoleums, the horror of which was deepened by the shadows of the night. They passed through two villages, almost deserted; ...and, at length arrived at the foot of the terrace of black marble ([27]).

Chardin ([28]) whose itinerary Vathek followed closely, had described the ruins of Istakar as made of black stone that was even harder than marble. Another traveller supplied the minute description of the ruins themselves :

> The moon dilated on a vast platform, the shades of the lofty columns which reached from the terrace almost to the clouds. The gloomy watch-towers, whose number could not be counted, were covered by no roof; and their capitals, of an architecture unknown in the records of the earth, served as an asylum for the birds of night, which alarmed at the approach of such visitants fled away croaking.
>
> ...Vathek ...presenting his hand to Nouronihar ; and, ascending the steps of a vast staircase, reached the terrace, which was flagged with squares of marble, and resembled a smooth expanse of water, upon whose surface not a blade of grass ever dared to vegetate. On the right rose the watch-towers, ranged before the ruins of an immense palace, whose walls were compassed with various figures. In front stood forth the colossal forms of four creatures, composed of the leopard and the griffin, and though but of stone, inspired emotions of terror.

The passage was a faithful description of engravings printed in Le Brun's *Voyage par la Moscovie en Perse* (1718 ([29])), except that the author of *Vathek* had multiplied the colossal animal forms from two into four and added an uncanny sense of terror

---

(27) *An Arabian Tale* (1786), 187.

(28) Chardin, Jean. *Voyage en Perse et autres lieux de l'Orient*, London, 1668, Amsterdam, 1711.

(29) For detailed comparison see May, M. *op. cit.*, 300 ff.

by the realisation that there was the end of Vathek's quest, and the expectation of the appearance of the Giaour at any moment.

The tradition that there were subterranean premises under the ruins of Istakhar, which people commonly believed to be full of treasure, had also been reported by the same two travellers. But Vathek and Nouronihar were soon to discover that those subterranean premises not only harboured the coveted treasures but were in themselves Hell, where daring culprits were tormented by the very achievment of their wishes. This last turn in the aspect of the subterranean hoards was completely incompatible with the genuine oriental folk imagination that produced the tradition.

The picture of Solomon as an inhabitant (though a temporary one) of Eblis's domains, could not possibly have been conceived by a true believing Moslem. The Islamic tradition was that Soliman-Ben-Daoud was a good and favoured prophet of God. His mastery overy animal, bird and Jinn was rather a mark of God's very high favour; the number of his wives and concubines was no sin by oriental standards. Nevertheless, the writer was certainly very well versed in oriental lore, particularly the *Arabian Nights,* where the Prophet or King Soliman plays such a prominent part with his ring, his magic carpet, his bed and his numerous slaves among the Jinn, imprisoned for thousands of years in small phials at the bottom of the sea.

Only a late nineteenth century orientalist, with a wide knowledge and deep affection for things Arabian like Victor Chauvin, could see the book as a monstrous imitation and express his dislike for it more than once. In his highly appreciative review of M.P. Conant's work he remarked on the subject of *Vathek* :

> Quant à *Vathek,* exalté partout en Angleterre..., Mlle Conant n'a pas pu s'abstenir de suivre la mode et elle l'a loué aussi. Mais, dans le détail, elle le juge très sévèrement et, en général nous serons d'accord avec elle. ([30])

---

(30) Chauvin, Victor. "*The Oriental Tale in England in the Eighteenth Century,* by Martha Pike Conant...", *Extrait de la Revue de l'Instruction Publique en Belgique,* n.d., p. 256.

Apparently, the wide display of 'Arabian' learning in the copious notes could not deceive the learned orientalist at the distance of over a century.

The Notes of *Vathek* :—

*The History of the Caliph Vathek,* as originally published in 1786, was accompanied by a most "formidable array of notes", certainly unprecedented in an oriental tale of the eighteenth century. For material, the notes drew extensively on the greater number of publications, in any way connected with the East, so far published. They were undoubtedly less numerous than those cited in later 'tales' as, for example, *Lalla Rookh* (1817), but they were in most cases more to the point. For the name of the Caliph and his anscetors in the very opening sentence, the reader was promptly referred to D'Herbelot, and the names of one book after another followed in rapid succession.

Almost all the sources of information on the still fabulous East, available in 1786, were mentioned and lavishly quoted. Picart's *Religious Ceremonies* (1723) ([31]) explained Indian deities like Ixora and Vishnoo mentioned in the text. Sale's translation of the Koran and above all the *Preliminary Discourse* (1734) ([32]) supplied sufficient illustrations of Islamic religion. Richardson's *Dissertation* (1777) illustrated mythological allusions to the Simurgh or "the mountain called Kaf" and for one thing supplied the famous "Carbuncle of Giamschid". Sir William Jones's translations from Persian, Turkish or Arabic poetry ([23]) were

---

(31) Picart, Bernard. *Ceremonies et Coutumes Religieuses de Tous Les Peuples du Monde*, 9 Tomes, fol. Amsterdam, 1723. An English translation as *The Ceremonies and Religious Customs of the Various Nations of the Known World... with a large number of Folio Copper Plates...*, 7 vols. was issued London, 1733.

(32) Sale, George, *The Koran...* To which is prefixed *A Preliminary Discourse*, London, 1734. One of the main sources of information on the Islamic faith in the 18th century.

(33) Jones, William. *Poems Consisting Chiefly of Translations from the Asiatic Languages*, London, 1772, a slender volume of adaptations rather than 'translations', was lavishly quoted in the *Notes*. For the simple picture of Nouronihar's hair "floating in the breeze", the editor quoted a couplet from *Solima* (an alleged Arabian eclogue), then followed two pages of reference to classical authorities, winding up with a Biblical reference and a final quotation from the preface of the same *Poems, An Arabian Tale* (1786), 234-7.

quoted more often as an embellishment, though the editor or translator (allegedly from the Arabic), managed to find some sort of pretext, often very weak, for bringing them in. The Moallakat ([34]) were copiously quoted, strangely enough, to illustrate details in the life of a most sophisticated Caliph who enjoyed, besides the wealth of the rich valley of the Tigris and the Euphrates, the legacy of the ancient civilisation of the Persian Empire. Stanzas were quoted from *Solima*, from the famous Persian Song ([35]) of Hafiz and the Turkish ode on the love of the nightingale for those rose. Lady Mary Wortley Montagu's *Letters from Turkey* supplied illustrations of domestic details and the interior arrangement of the harem of the Emir Fakreddin where Nouronihar was the adored despot. But it was to the *Arabian Nights* that the editor most frequently turned. The *Arabian Nighs* together with the *Tales of Inatulla* (1768), supplied illustrations of every kind, ranging from spoons of cocknos to the multi-coloured fish which Carathis bewitched into speaking of the whereabouts of Gulchenrouz. The editor was certainly a great enthusiast of the *Arabian Nights*; he asserted their authenticity and quoted the testimony of Colonel Capper that was to form an important item of many an introduction to the *Arabian Nights* in the nineteenth century. It was probably the editor of *Vathek* who first drew attention to the traveller's

---

([34]) Sir William Jones's translation of the *Moallakat* or *Seven Poems of the Arabians* was 1st published in London 1783. The author of *Vathek* speaking of how "vigilant guards (of the Caliph's cavalcade) having remarked certain cages of ladies swagging somewhat awry, discovered that a few adventurous gallants had contrived to get in", clearly had a passage from the poem of Amriolkais in mind :

«On tha happy day I entered the carriage, the carriage of ONEIZA who said... (*While the vehicle was bent aside with our weight*).
"O AMRIOLKAIS, descend or my best also will be killed." Jones, *Works* (1807), X, 10,-11.

The editor of the *Notes*, however, did not once refer to this particular poem, but to the poems of Lebeid and Zohair (3rd and 4th poems of the Moallakat) to illustrate the way women travelled in general.

([35]) *An Arabian Tale* (1786), 237

comparison of the *Nights* to *Don Quixote*. (36) The editor kept up the pretence of a translation from the Arabic by sometimes singling out a certain phrase, analysing it in the notes and commenting on its superior beauty in the original. To give a final touch of the same effect before the end, he chose the word 'brotherhood' in a context in the text and pretended that there was a lacuna in the original transcript of the text and that he had supplied the words as the most suitable to the meaning. The evidence of travellers quoted in the notes foreshadowed the extensive use which Southey, Moore and to some extent Byron, made of the growing number of travellers' accounts of the East.

Besides the display of great erudition on subjects oriental, to some extent, justified by the alleged Arabian origin of the *Tale,* the notes showed a wide knowledge of classical and Biblical lore. Learned discussions on passages from Euripides and Milton were followed by homely details from the Letters of Lady M.W. Montagu concerning the "Mecoa balm" — a beauty appliance used by ladies in Turkey — and other details of oriental ladies' toilet. (37)

A careful reader of the notes might have detected the French origin of the tale. The editor sometimes at a loss to account for a seemingly ambiguous phrase in the English translation, alleged in the notes that the idiom was very difficult to express in English, but that the French language seemed more suitable for an accurate rendering of the original Arabic. Thus

> ...my senses are dazled with the radiance that beams from thy charms (38),

which seemed rather too long and vague for the gallant compliment, it was supposed to be, was explained in French in the notes as

> ...thy countenance, Rayonnante de beautés et de grâces... (to express an idiom for which we have no substitute). (39)

---

(36) Colonel Capper's observations on the *Arabian Nights* were quoted in full, *ibid.*, 379-381.
(37) *Ibid.*, 282-4.
(38) *Ibid.*, 103.
(39) *Ibid.*, 286.

Other cases in which

> The original... (was) more analogous to the French than the English idiom ([40]),

were numerous but they seem to have passed unnoticed and reviewers took the editor at his word concerning the origin of the tale.

*The Gentleman's Magazine* commenting on the preface remarks:

> The pleasure and information which this specimen of the collection has afforded us cannot but excite an eager desire for the communication of the rest. ([41])

One suspects that the reviewer had not really managed to examine the book with care (the book was published on 7th June and the review was in the July number of the magazine). The story was described as "generally vivid and elegant". The two closing paragraphs of the tale were quoted as one recapitulated the story and saved the reviewer the labour of summarising it, and the other described the terrible punishment of Vathek and his beloved Nouronihar for their insolence in attempting to transgress the boundaries of human knowledge. It was the only 'moral' passage in the tale and was thus convenient for quotation. Of the elaborate notes, the last one was singled out for quotation and the reviewer having discharged his duty towards the tale of the *Caliph Vathek,* turned to what had really interested him in the whole work. Towards the end of the notes the editor, commenting on

> "the abode of vengeance and despair", ([42])

in which the culprits were condemned to wander to eternity, quoted Dante's description of the inscription on the gates of Hell. An English translation by W. Hayley followed and an observation between parentheses on,

---

(40) *Ibid.*, 305.
(41) *The Gentleman's Magazine*, LVI (July, 1786), 593.
(42) *An Arabian Tale...* (1786), 200.

> How much have the Public to regret after the Specimen given, that Mr. Hayley does not compleat the INFERNO (43).

It was there that the reviewer found himself on familiar ground and proceeded to second the editor's regrets and discuss the relative merits of various measures and the best way of adapting Dante's triplet to the English distich. To wind up he recommended *Vathek* "for the morality of the design".

"The labours of the editor" were praised in the highest terms, the notes were found to

> ...abound with various examples of the most refined taste, and the most extensive erudition. (44)

So the new *Arabian Tale* was favourably received and the editor looked round for opportunities of advertising his production and drawing the attention of men of letters to himself. In the number of the following January, a frequent correspond to the *Gentleman's Magazine* on Classical questions, who signed his letters S.W. volunteered a long commentary (45) on a line of Virgil in one of the longest of learned notes. The editor and translator of the *Arabian Tale* had taken the opportunity of the appearance of "a vast wood of palm trees" in the text, to embark on a long discussion of a line by Virgil which mentioned the palm trees. The line had roused some controversy in translation and the learned editor exhibited his own erudition in some five or six pages (46) that had nothing at all to do with the History of the Caliph Vathek. The correspondent of the *Gentleman's Magazine* was mainly interested in the discussion on Virgil and dismissed the tale in which it occurred wth a conjecture that,

> ...it should seem, (it) ———has been composed as a text, for the purpose of giving to the public the information contained in the notes (47)

---

(43) *Ibid.*, 332.

(44) *The Gentleman's Magazine, op. cit.*, 594.

(45) Stephen Weston (1747-1830), an antiquary and man of letters, who later became an orientalist of numerous but rather eccentric publications.

(46) *An Arabian Tale...* (1786), 269 ff.

(47) *The Gentleman's Magazine*, LVII (January, 1787), 55.

He referred to the editor as "the author" throughout the discussion so we infer that he considered the work to be a pseudo-translation but was not interested in pursuing the subject.

The translator answered in the following number coyly asserting that,

> ...the said History, is, as the preface declares, a translation of an unpublished manuscript, which Mr. W. himself will be welcome to examine. (48)

He did not, however, insist on the manuscript being Arabic. He proceeded to draw certain conclusions from Mr. W.'s letter, all flattering to himself which Mr. W. certainly did not intend:

> The first is, that Mr. W. judging from the *notes*, thinks the writer of them equal to the composition of the *text*. The second, that since the translation has passed with Mr. W. for an original it must have some pretention to favour. And the third, that the notes are more apposite to the text than might have been looked for...

That the Rev. Samuel Henley (1740-1815) seemed to derive so much satisfaction from the inference that the writer of the notes was equal to the composition of the text and that the translation was so good that it could pass for an original, has a roguish ring of truth, which only the modern reader can understand, after the numerous, and to a great extent, successful attempts at clearing up the mysteries that attended the publication of the enigmatic *Vathek*. To the majority of readers of the *Gentleman's Magazine* (1787), the coyly worded, evasive reply carried none of those meanings. But, in one reader at least, and that the true author of *Vathek*, it must have evoked a terrible storm of rage, the more violent because of its impotance before the little clergyman's treachery.

\* \* \*

---

(48) *Ibid.*, 120.

## II

> One day at a very early age he came across a copy of the *Arabian Nights* and this chance find had more effect upon his life and character than any other incident. He read and reread these stories with avidity, and the impression they made on him was so strong that Lord Chatham instructed Lettice that the book must be kept from him. The precaution came too late... the Oriental tales had taken possession of the impressionable reader... They had fired his youthful mind and held his imagination captive ; their influence over him never waned all the days of his life, (Lewis Melville, *Life and Letters of William Beckford of Fonthill*, London, Heinmann, 1910, p. 20.)

It is not my intention to add to the numerous studies of the career, character, eccentricities or perversions of the author of *Vathek*. Only two aspects of the personal history of William Beckford should interest us here : first, what the oriental setting of the *Tale* meant for the young author, and second, the effect of his own career on the fame and influence of the book.

The first of these two aspects was first studied in detail by Marcel May in 1928. [49] This highly enthusiastic work was rather guardedly received by more conservative English scholars, [50] on account of the large amount of guesswork that formed its foundation. Subsequent research by Beckford scholars has now corrected, besides corroborating and supplementing, many of M. May's findings. Much of the data of Beckford's life revealed by J.W. Oliver, [51] Professor Guy

---

(49) May, Marcel. *La jeunesse de William Beckford et la génèse de son Vathek*, Paris, 1928.

(50) See Ernest Baker's review of the book in the *Review of English Studies*, V (1929), 235-271.

(51) Oliver, J. W. *The Life of William Beckford*, London, Oxford University Press, 1932.

Chapman (⁵²) and later by Mr. Boyd Alexander (⁵³) would have been a great help to M. May. Without this additional valuable data, however, he had followed the right scent in evaluating *Vathek* as a "rôle de vision" rather than "a satire on unlimited power... (and as such) ...an eighteenth century common place", (⁵⁴) as often alleged by nineteeth century critics. The talented young man who conceived the Caliph Vathek was the last man in the world to write "a satire on unlimited power". M. May has shown to what extent the character of Vathek, was a projection of Beckford's own. When the Commander of the Faithful singed the beards of his worthy subjects, shocked the holy men with his irreverence or caused sermon-preaching nuisances to be pinched to death, he was, the writer thought, avenging the thousand petty vexations which the vulgarity of Frangistan caused the passionate autocrat of Fonthill. (⁵⁵) The Caliph's fondness for fresh meadows and lofty mountains and the fascination he entertained for the moon, particularly when it was full, were all in keeping with the character of young Beckford, fresh after his tour in Switzerland and his youthful enthusiasm for Mount Salève. (⁵⁶)

---

(52) Guy Chapman's biography of William Beckford was first published in 1937. The edition to which all references in this essay have been made is that re-issued in *The Life and Letter Series* (No. 98), 1940. A new edition was published by Rupert Hart-Davis, London, 1952. It is exactly similar to that of 1940 except for a short second preface by the author in which he corrected a few errors in the older edition and revoked his verdict of not guilty, concerning the charge of Beckford's homosexuality. Apart from that the new edition is merely a re-issue of that of 1940.

(53) Alexander, Boyd. (edit) *The Journal of William Beckford in Portugal and Spain*, 1787-1788, London, Rupert Hart-Davis, 1954.
— *Life at Fonthill, 1807-1822. With Interludes in Paris and London, From the Correspondence of William Beckford*, London, Rupert Hart-Davis, 1957.

(54) Saintsbury, George. *A History of Nineteenth Century Literature*, 1780-1895, London, Macmillan, 1896, p. 40.

(55) May, M. *op.cit.*, 188.

(56) See Beckford's letters from Switzerland in Lewis Melville's, *Life and Letters of William Beckford of Fonthill*, London, Heinmann, 1910.

The Palace of the Five Senses, dwelling of the exotic Caliph, was analysed by the writer in this fashion :

> Sorti des hombres de l'histoire, pour devenir 'rôle de vision,' le Caliph Vathek habite donc une demeure que l'imagination de William a faite pièce à pièce en pillant à travers l'Europe ici une colonnade, un péri-style, là une tour qu'il agrandit comme font les clairs de lune, partout des souvenirs de grandeur et de beauté. ([57])

Furthermore, the palace and the tower were certainly an anticipation of what Beckford tried to realize for himself later in life, when he was thwarted in his ambitions for a peerage. The passion and haste with which he built the tower at Fonthill and later the tower at Lansdown, though his fortune was almost broken by such extravagance, all show that the tower where Vathek and his mother watched the stars and sacrificed to the powers of darkness, meant much more to the author than one might guess from merely reading the book, without the necessary knowledge of the man who wrote it. ([58])

May's analysis of the other characters of the tale in relation to members of Beckford's own family adds much interest to the book, though it finally adds nothing to its literary evaluation. Carathis becomes more interesting when understood to have been modelled on Beckford's mother, "The Begum" as he called her, Morakanabad as the Rev. John Lettice, Beckford's mild tutor and Nouronihar as Louisa Beckford, his cousin Peter's wife who certainly was no paragon of virtue, and who would sacrifice everything and everybody from her husband to her son to gratify the least wish of her "sweet William",

As facts concerning "Kitty" i.e. William Courtnay, revealed by Oliver and Chapman, had not yet come to light, M. May took the effeminate Gulchenrouz for a representation of Beckford's own innocent childhood. Ernest Baker, though differing with the French writer on many points agreed with him on this :

---

(57) May, M. *op.cit.*, 209.

(58) For a study of Beckford and the houses and towers he built, see Brockman, H.A.N. *The Caliph of Fonthill*, Werner Laurie, London, 1956.

...there is more than one reflex of Beckford in the tale. The Caliph with his unscrupulous and insatiable ambition typifies his exorbitant egoism and boundless curiosity; the amiable Gulchenrouz mirrors the easy-going epicurean side of Beckford's nature. But the infernal potentate Eblis, and the tortured Solomon, brooding over the annihilation of his earthly grandeur, are likewise drawn from the future autocrat of Fonthill. ([59])

The vast analysis of the work in relation to Beckford's own personality seems to justify the author's final comment that *Vathek* was:

Œuvre d'enthousiasme, d'impulsif, livrant au jeu des circonstances le fruit de son imagination... Œuvre qui dans les chemins du passé, arrête encore le regard comme l'un des monuments les plus curieux du romantisme à son aube, mais qui... se découvre sa vrai figure que si l'on veut observer la nature de ses matériaux et la pierre d'angle, autour de laquelle une loi d'affinité les groupa... le, Moi de l'auteur... (et)... les exigences secrètes que ce moi manifeste et satisfait dans la sphère imaginative. ([60])

This final commentary which sums up the writer's thesis throughout the study does not imply that "The oriental features of *Vathek* are accidental", as Professor Baker concludes. On the contrary the number of books which Beckford had studied or simply read before composing the tale, shows to what extent his mind was impregnated with travellers' lore, tales translated or compiled, all concerning the East, which represented for him what the splendour of Mogul architecture in the Pavilion of Brighton meant for the Prince Regent in 1817. ([61]) Evidence showing the large number of works behind *Vathek* itself, was derived partly from Beckford's hints about his own readings in

---

(59) Baker, Ernest. *op. cit.*, 240.
(60) May, M. *op. cit.*, 414.
(61) See Musgrave, Clifford. *Royal Pavilion, A Study in the Romantic*, Brighton, 1951.

letters written before 1786, (⁶²) from lists of books in the sale of his Fonthill library in 1823, but mainly from the correspondence with Samuel Henley during the course of 1785-1786. Henley was engaged in translating *Vathek* into English and in compiling the extensive notes of the *Arabian Tale* and Beckford gave him specific instructions where to turn for illustrations. In answer to the bewildered clergyman's queries he wrote : (⁶³)

>...The Arabian Nights will furnish some illustrations (particularly as to Ghouls, etc.) but much more may be learnt from Herbelot's Bib[liothèque] Orient[ale] and Richardson's Diss[ertation].
>
> April 23, 1785. (⁶⁴)

or

>The Domes of Shaddukian and Amberabad you will find explained in Richardson.
>
>The Cocknos is a bird whose bill is much esteemed in Persia for its beautiful polish, and sometimes used as a spoon ; see Persian Tales, Hist. of the Sorrowful Vizir, and Zelica Begum.

---

(62) See Melville, Lewis, *op.cit.*, particularly letters to Cozens and Lady Hamilton. A letter probably to Cozens, written December 4th, 1778, shows to what extent Beckford's mind was impregnated with travellers' accounts of Eastern countries, even at that early date. The letter headed with "Being the full of the moon:" describes a dream Beckford had, sitting on a cushion by the fire, like orientals, after a long solitary walk : "Meanwhile my thoughts were wandering into the interior of Africa and dwelt for hours on those countries I love. Strange tales of Mount Atlas and relations of Travellers amused my fancy. One instant, I imagined myself viewing the marble palaces of Ethiopian princes... Some few minutes after, I found myself standing before a thick wood listneing to impetuous water falls... a tall comely Negro wound along the slopes of the Hills and without moving his lips made me comprehend I was in Africa, on the brink of the Nile beneath the mountains of Amara..., *ibid*, 63.

(63) The correspondence is published in Melville *op.cit.*, but they are conveniently grouped together in Lewis Melville's introduction to *The Episodes of Vathek*, tr. by Sir Frank T. Marzials, Stephen Swift and Co..., London, 1912, from which my quotations are taken.

(64) *Ibid.*, p. XIV.

> The butterflies of Cachemire are celebrated in a poem of Memphis!! I slaved at with Zemir, the old Mohammedan, who assisted me in translating W. Montagu's MSS. But they are hardly worth a note.
>
> I suppose you will prepare a tolerably long note on the Simorgue. That respectable bird deserves all you can say of her. Soliman Raad, Soliman Daki (not Dawmin's, for God's sake) and Soliman surnamed Gian-ben-Gian will furnish ample scope for a display of oriental conditions. (65)

This correspondence in some respects reminds the reader of the short hurried notes exchanged between Byron and John Murray, during the publication of the *Turkish Tales* almost thirty years later. (66) In the letter quoted above, Beckford strangely enough used the term "costume" in exactly the same sense and context as Byron. Beckford told Henley in 1785, "I believe in most respects I have been exact in my costume". Byron writing to Professor Clarke, the traveller in 1813 said,

> ...you have seen and described more of the East than any of your predecessors... you are one of the very few men who can pronounce how far my costume (to use an affected but expressive word) is correct. (67)

Byron had certainly not read Beckford's letter to Henley but the parallel shows that Beckford was as scrupulous concerning "correctness of costume", as the nineteenth century contributors to the oriental tale.

\* \* \*

---

(65) *Ibid.*, p. XVII.

(66) One letter of Byron to Murray, on Dec. 3, 1813 ran:
"...Look out the Encyclopedia article *Mecca* whether it is there or at *Medina* the Prophet is entombed, if at Medina the first lines of my alteration must run..." *Letters and Journals*, II, 298.
... Apparently receiving no answer he again wrote. "Did you look out? Is it *Medina* or *Mecca* that contains the holy Sepulcre? don't make me blaspheme by your negligence I have no books of reference or I would save you the trouble", *loc. cit.*

(67) *Ibid.*, 308-9.

> ...a work bearing the marks of a transition period. (68)

*Vathek* does mark "the swing over from classicism to romanticism" but more specifically from the oriental tale of the eighteenth century to that of the nineteenth. Beckford had one great advantage over many of the later contributors to the oriental tale who had either been on the spot or had massive sources of information at their disposal. He had acquired a knowledge of Arabic (though Cyrus Redding suspected it was only a smattering of Persian). (69) Guy Chapman's examination of the Beckford papers resulted in the revelation of a large number of translations from the *Arabian Nights* and other E.W. Montagu manuscripts which Beckford seems to have translated into French, partly as an exercise in language. (70) Thus Beckford was actually able to read much of the *Arabian Nights* in the original. His impatience, however, (he was only twenty-one at the time) and his own fiery imagination disqualified him for any scholarly achievement in the field of faithful translation. Guy Chapman found besides the translations, manuscripts of at least six tales, many including frame tales in which the author or translator largely deviated from the original. As Chapman remarks,

> ...only a deeply versed Oriental scholar could distinguish which of the doubtful tales are original and which translations...

The preface which Beckford himself wrote to one of these tales (probably at a later date) indicates the way most of them

---

(68) Chapman, Guy., and Hodgkin, John. *A Bibliography of William Beckford of Fonthill*, London,, Constable, 1930, p. XVIII.

(69) During a visit to Paris 1814, Beckford vaunted of having made a great impression on L.M. Launglès, the French orientalist by his pronunciation of Arabic and Persian (!), B. Alexander, *Life at Fonthill*, 160.

(70) *cf. supra*, p. 17, n. 5. Dr. A. Parreaux's *William Beckford, Auteur de 'Vathek'*, Paris (1960), received at the time of printing gives a more detailed account of these papers.

took shape. The tale was *Histoire d'Elouard Felkanaman et d'Ansel Hougioud* which was apparently his version of the story of *Ons-el-Wogood and Rose-bud The Vizier's Daughter* from the *Arabian Nights*. The preface reported by Chapman ran:

> ...J'avais, commencé à traduire litéralement. Mon maître d'arabe, un vieux musulman né natif de Mecque, me l'avois recommendé comme exercise de langue — J'ai trouvé pourtant la narration si pompeusement ennuieuse que je l'ai jetté de côté — Zemir voulut me brider comme de raison mais ayant pris le mord aux dents, je me suis emporté à grand galop dans les régions de ma propre imagination — voici le résultat... [71]

The large number of translations (exercises), considering the short period in which (according to G. Chapman), they must have been undertaken, testifies to the vigour with which Beckford flung himself into these studies, when he came of age. The old restrictions exacted by his guardians and his tutor had apparently only increased his infatuation with the *Arabian Nights* His eccentric drawing master had secretly supplied him with ample material to keep up his preference for the forbidden literature. Beckford later told Cyrus Redding,

> I preferred it (oriental literature) to the classics of Greece and Rome. I began it myself as a relief from the *dryness* of my other studies... The Latin and Greek were set tasks. The Persian I began of my own accord. [72]

Even credulous old Cyrus Redding could see clearly why this literature seemed so attractive to young Beckford:

> ...there is no doubt that having flung off the rule of tutors and guardians, he expatiated freely in oriental lore, His favourite literaturer which he studied furtively before he was of age, and the love of which remained with him to the last. The arbitrary power of the rulers of the East,

---

(71) *A Bibliography of William Beckford*, 93.
(72) (Redding, Cyrus.) *Memoirs of William Beckford of Fonthill, Author of Vathek*, London, Charles Skeet, 1859, II, 243.

and the obsequiousness of their subjects, seemed congenial to his notions of that magnificence, which accompanying power, had delighted him in his early reading, and caused the remonstrances of his tutor, and cautions from the Earl of Chatham. (73)

Thus the significance of the oriental vogue as supplying one of the outlets for early Romantic revolt, is well illustrated by the infatuation of the young millionnaire, chafing under a thousand restrictions, exacted by his aristocratic relatives. This may very well explain the fascination which both *Vathek* and its author had for that most outspoken of Romantic Rebels, Byron.

## *VATHEK* and *THE VISION* :—

At the age of seventeen the godson of Chatham was already determined in his revolt against the classical well balanced education that was to make a statesman and a politician of the hope of the house. He wrote from Switzerland (October, 3rd. 1777) probably to his mentor, the "Archangel", his eccentric drawing master.

> To receive visits and to return them, to be mighty civil, well-bred, quiet, prettily dressed and smart is to be what your old ladies call in England a charming gentleman... To pay and receive fulsome compliments from the learned, to talk with modesty and precision, to sport an opinion gracefully..., to delight in mathematics, logick, geometry and the rule of Right,... to despise poetry and venerable antiquity, murder taste, abhor imagination, detest all the charms of eloquence unless capable of mathematical demonstration, and more than all to be vigourously incredulous, is to gain the reputation of good sense. Such an animal I am sometimes doomed to be! To glory in horses, to know how to knock up and how to cure them, to smell of the stable, swear, talk bawdy, eat roast beef, drink, speak bad French... Such an animal I am determined not to be! (74)

---

(73) *Ibid.*, II, 212.
(74) Melville, Lewis, *op.cit.*, 31.

Instead of being a gentleman, "comme il faut", as he had said in the last letter, the young man was wandering on shaggy mountains, falling more deeply under the influence of Rousseau and Voltaire. Of the reading that formed his imagination at that impressionable age, G. Chapman writes:

> ...with a good knowledge of Latin, Greek, Persian, Arabic and Sanskrit, (75) [!], his reading had embraced not only the classical authors, but also the writings of the Romantic Movement, which in 1777 had firmly fixed itself on the imagination of Europe. Ossian had captured him, and "my favourite" the melancholy Gray. With these, with Dante and Ariosto with volumes on Northern mythology, on travels in China, India and Mexico, with the *Arabian Nights* and other Oriental Tales... he had more than enough to inflame his active mind. These and the mountains inspired him. (76)

The result was a strange composition which he called "my Centrical History", composed in "a chamber thirty feet large", which he sent to his mentor, instructing him not to show it to anyone as most people were "different from us", and would only ridicule the precious effusions of the young man. His well-balanced relatives would indeed have been surprised at the composition of the young man, whom they had sent to the Continent to finish a classical education with the classical Grand-Tour. They, who six years later forced him to suppress the whole edition *of Dreams, Waking Thoughts, and Incidents,* (1783), would certainly have committed *The Vision* to the same fire as *The Arabian Nights*.

*The Vision* survived in manuscript, however, or at least part of it to be resurrected in 1930 by Guy Chapman who gave it

---

(75) It is highly improbable that Beckford should have had any knowledge of Sanskrit in 1777. He had probably read Anquetil Du Perron's *Zend-Avesta*, Paris, 1770, and Abraham Roger's account of the Hindus in Picart's *Religious Ceremonies*, 1723, but no more.

(76) Beckford, William. *The Vision* and *Liber Veritatis*, ed. Guy Chapman London, Constable, 1930 p. XIII.

this title. This remarkable performance, astonishing indeed for a boy of seventeen, is mainly interesting to us in relation to *Vathek*. Scenes and characters of Beckford's major work germinated in this early composition. The narrator wandering by himself up untrodden mountain paths on a moonlit night, is met by two majestic figures a Brahmin (who later turns into an angel), Moisasour and a maiden draped in muslins who is called Nouronihar. Her eyes are sometimes described as blue, sometimes green and sometimes black. He sometimes describes her as "the fair Indian" but at other times she seems to be Persian and "the Persian language sounded most sweetly from her lips." Her character is totally different from the Caliph Vathek's bride, for she is all goodness and wisdom. The manuscript ends with her giving the narrator, who has just passed through most impossible ordeals, a meal composed of the milk of cocoas and the juice of a thousand fruits and settling down to read to him from two large volumes covered with mystic writings.

The scene of the Hall of Eblis is to some extent anticipated in *The Vision*. The author after passing the trials that proved him worthy of the company and education of the good Brahmin, arrives in company with two angel-like creatures (Malick and Terminga), at the throne of Moisasour :

> ...We arrived at a vast arch closed by a portal of ebony, whose valves flying open of a sudden with a sound that rang amongst the alters, displayed an immensely spacious concave unsupported by any visible cause and glowing with a refulgence that proceeded from an orb of the most brilliant hue, suspended from the centre by chains that, almost imperceptible, wore the appearance of sunbeams. Under the orb I beheld a flight of many hundred steps covered with a rich carpet of purple which imitated the mossy herbage of the subterranean valleys. On every step sat a lucid form increasing in glory and stature, the nearer they approached Moisasour who was seated on the summit of the steps while Nouronihar reclined at his feet. ([77])

---

(77) *Ibid.*, 38.

The resemblance between this scene and the description of the Hall of Eblis quoted above is too evident to need any commentary. The difference lies in the feeling of luminous wisdom and natural goodness that pervades the whole atmosphere of *The Vision,* much in contrast to the sense of evil that hangs over *Vathek.* Lockhart, writing of *Vathek* in 1834, in the belief that "it was written... and published before the author closed his twentieth year" (a mistake common enough at the time), might have derived some comfort from the sense of Beckford's 'innocence' at that early age, had he been given a glimpse of *The Vision.* Lockhart's main criticism of *Vathek* was that,

> The boy-author appears already to have rubbed the bloom off his heart ; and in the midst of his dazzling genius, one trembles to think that a stripling of years so tender should have attained the cool cynicism of a Candide. ([78])

## THE EPISODES OF VATHEK :—

It is even more interesting to carry the same comparison to the *Episodes* which Beckford had intended as companion pieces to *Vathek* ([79]) in order to give the work the same form of many tales within a tale, as the *Arabian Nights.*

*The Episodes* which Beckford revised, polished and rounded, continuously during his long years of isolation, reveal a most disquieting depth of cool criminality, surpassing even the

---

(78) *The Quarterly Review,* LI (1834), p. 427.

(79) The work as Beckford had intended it, was first published by Guy Chapman in 1929 :

Beckford, William of Fonthill. *Vathek with The Episodes of Vathek.* ed. with a Historical Introduction and Notes by Guy Chapman, Cambridge, Constable..., 1929. The edition is in French as the editor regards "the only form for an authoritative edition of the whole is that designed by the author". *The Episodes* were put aside after Henley's breech of faith by the separate publication of *Vathek,* 1786 and were published for the first time in 1912, in the translation of Sir Frank T. Marzials mentioned above.

wickedness of the Caliph. That explains why they remained unpublished even after *Vathek* had attained great popularity. ([80]) Publishers shied at the disturbing work and found sufficient excuse in the author's unreasonable demands. ([81])

*The Episodes* would provide a good subject for the study of Beckford's adapting the oriental setting for a display of the worst depths of evil to which human beings can sink. As they never saw the light before 1912, they remained one of the mysterious literary curiosities of the nineteenth century. Beckford would favour one of the few visitors who had access to Fonthill Abbey, or later to the court of Lansdown Bagdad, with a sight of one or more of the *Episodes* and the visitor would spread the rumour to the outside world. ([82]) The author would certainly have published them if he could ; he mentioned them in the preface to the French edition of *Vathek*, issued in 1815 :

---

(80) Beckford wrote in 1832 to George Clarke, his agent :
"As to the Episodes of Vathek"... Murray or Colburn or Longman, or any body might have had them ; at a moment too when any sense or nonesense connected with Fonthill Abbey would have run through edition after edition like wildfire. But not seeing their way so clearly as might have been imagined, they neglected the opening, and shrunk back from one of the best speculations of the kind that ever presented itself", *The Episodes of Vathek*, *ed. cit.*, p. XXX.

(81) Beckford probably reflecting on the three thousand guineas Moore got for *Lalla Rookh* (1817) wrote to Clarke in 1833 :
"Unless Bentley can persuade himself, and feels inspired, to give a sum as round as the great globe itself, nay, rounder — for the globe we know is flatter at the poles than my Episodes, I hope, will be found in any part of them — we are not likely to deal. As you... write me positive word in yesterday's letter that he will never think of thousands, he had better give up the point..." *ibid.*, XXXI.

(82) Samuel Rogers was one of the few literary men of the age allowed within the high walls of Fonthill Abbey during Beckford's residence there. Beckford read to him two of *The Episodes* and he cunningly wrote to Byron of the *Story of Kalilah and Zulkais*, the brother and sister whose incestuous passion for each other finally landed them in the Palace of Subterranean Fire. Byron in his exile (1818), was deeply interested and begged to be allowed a sight of the curious tales, but Beckford declined.

> J'ai préparé quelques Episodes ; ils sont indiqués, à la page 200, comme faisant suite à Vathek — peut-être paroîtront-ils un jour. (83).

An advertisement for an edition of *Vathek* with the *Episodes* in French was found among the Beckford papers at Hamilton Palace. It was clearly written at some later date for it mentioned the popularity of *Don Juan* as an excuse for publishing the *Episodes* :

> Depuis quelque tems nous avançons à pas précipités vers la tolérance universelle. Le fameux drama d'Horace Walpole, fondé sur l'inceste le plus révoltant, se publie enfin sans scruple. On dévore « Don Juan », on se jette à corps perdu sur les romans de Madame du Devant (George Sand) et de Victor Hugo... j'ose me flatter qu'au moins *la morale* de mes contes est assez évidente pour produire des réflexions salutaires... (84)

Even these reflexions were apparently not strong enough to appease the qualms of squeamish publishers of the century and the *Episodes* never saw the light during the author's life and for over sixty years after his death.

Anyway, the *Caliph Vathek* was there in print, though deprived of his equally damned companions (85) and the nineteenth century recognised him and sometimes expressed great enthusiasm for him. Harriet Martineaux exclaimed *"Vathek* remains !"* and it has remained to our own day.

\* \* \*

---

(83) Beckford, William, *Vathek*, A Londres, Chez Clarke, 1815, preface dated 1st June, 1815.
(84) *The Episodes of Vathek*, etc., p. XXIX.
(85) It is interesting to note that Beckford once composed an *Episode of of the Story of Motassem* the Father of Vathek, which he seems to have destroyed completely, B. Alexander, *Life at Fonthill*, p. 182.

## III

Had *Vathek* had its chance in 1786 it is conceivable that it might have had a considerable following among the novelists of the day, *(A Bibliography of William Beckford,* p. XVIII).

There were nine editions ([86]) of *Vathek* issued during the author's life (according to Chapman's *Bibliography*) and innumerable editions since ([87]). The popularity of the work in the nineteenth century and the permanent place it has gained in the history of English literature must not, however, blind us to the the fact that the book had almost no influence at the time of its publication. In spite of the great importance attributed to

---

(86) An edition similar to the original edition of 1786 was published in 1809 as: *An Arabian Tale From An Unpublished Manuscript*, With Notes Critical and Explanatory, A New edition, London, printed for W. Clarke, 1809. Beckford's name was not mentioned.

The third edition was published as: *Vathek*. Translated from the Original French, 3rd ed., revised and corrected, London, Printed for W. Clarke, 1816. Beckford's name, though not mentioned on the title page, was mentioned inside and there is no doubt that this is the edition which the author himself completely authorised. It has been used as such in editions issued after his death. A fourth edition similar to the last was issued in 1823. In 1834, it was included in Bentley's *Standard Novels* with the *Castle of Otranto* and *The Bravo of Venice*.

(87) Editions of *Vathek* to this day present an astounding mixture of sense and nonsense. The most important edition issued before the end of the nineteenth century is that of Richard Garnett:

Beckford, William. *Vathek : An Arabian Tale*, ed., by Richard Garnett, with notes by Samuel Henley, and etchings by Herbert Nye, London, 1893. In his introduction Dr. Garnett refuted for the first time the story circulated by Beckford himself that he had composed *Vathek* 'at one sitting of three days and two nights, in which he never took off his clothes. Dr. Garnett proved that the composition must have taken at least a year. He revealed the role played by the Rev. Samuel Henley, whose name Beckford had always taken care to conceal (he told Redding that he did not know who translated the first edition and that it was tolerably done, Redding, *op.cit.*, I, 245). Garnett who had examined the collection of autograph letters in the possession of Mr. Morrison of Fonthill proved that the composition of the book had taken at least a year. He, however, exaggerated the part played by Henley in the whole performance. His views on this head were passionately combatted by May, *op. cit*.

it by Conant and many others, it must be admitted that this importance was not realized by readers for many years after the publication of the book. M.P. Conant has rightly given it a place in her study as the last important oriental tale of the eighteenth century, while we have given it prominence as the first and probably most important oriental tale of a new period (1786-1824). Marie de Meester classes it with the work of Sir William Jones and *The Arabian Nights* as one of the major sources of oriental influence in the literature of the nineteenth century. ([88]) Speaking of the influence of the tale on both Byron and Barry Cornwall she says :

> It is, however, not only through the fact, that those poets directly borrowed material from the work, that *Vathek* is so important, but also because it gave new food to the appetite for eastern literature, that had already been strong in the eighteenth century and thus forms a link between this century and the next. ([89])

As Marie de Meester was speaking of the whole course of the nineteenth century, her statement can very well be believed. It does not apply, however, to the early years of the nineteenth century, for *Vathek* was very little known for more than twenty-five years after its publication in 1786. Writers at the opening of this century often alleged that *Vathek* was very popular at the time of its publication. Paul Elmer More writing of Beckford in 1913 suspects,

> ...that *Vathek* is little read today,... But the book was popular in its time. ([90])

---

(88) Meester, Marie de. *Oriental Influences in the Literature of the Nineteenth Century*, Heidelberg, 1915.

(89) *Ibid.*, 21.

(90) More, Paul Elmer. *The Drift of Romanticism*, Shelburne Essays, 8th series, London, Constable and Co., 1913, p. 33.

See also for the same allegation the edition of *Vathek*, edited by Justin Hannaford, London, Greening and Co., 1900, (reprinted 1905). The editor, in spite of information already available in the French edition by Stephane Mallarme (1876) and Garnett's edition (1893), asserted that the book had made an immediate sensation both in England and France ! This was only one of numerous glaring mistakes of that editor, who had apparently taken the easy way to writing his introduction by merely recording current rumours on the now fabulous character of Beckford and his book.

G. Chapman's more realistic view is that,

> ...it cannot have been until the editions of 1815 and 1816 that the book began to have any kind of popularity... no one of importance had read it before Byron ([91]) found a copy and publicly testified to its merits. ([92])

This adequately accounts for the fact stressed by literary historians that the book had no impact on the course of the English novel. One must agree with what Sir Walter Raleigh wrote as early as 1907:

> This romance is infinitely finer than Walpole's Gothic toy, but it is less historically important. Walpole is a direct ancestor of Scott, while *Vathek*, unless Moore's much later *Epicurean* (1827) be affiliated to it, remained without distinguished progeny. ([93])

A later writer on the novel attributes this to the great success of the romances of Mrs. Anne Radcliffe. ([94])

It was not only the success of Mrs. Radcliffe, however, that decided the course of the current of the English novel at the time. One must remember that *Vathek* was virtually unknown:

> Even its name seems scarcely to have been known, Farrington speaks vaguely of a romance called "Vertax". ([95])

There is of course the possibility that even under different circumstances the book might have had little impact because of the alien nature of the oriental setting.

Any vogue or influence which the book might have had were strangled at birth. It was not a case where the edition

---

(91) Richard Garnett, in his introduction to *Vathek*, (1893) states that Southey read the book at least as early as 1806, while readers of *Thalaba* (1801) may suspect that he might have read it even earlier. Isaac D'Israeli read it sometime before 1799 when he referred to it in the notes of *The Loves of Mejnoun and Leila*, in *Romances* (1799)

(92) *A Bibliography of William Beckford...*, p. XVII.

(93) Raleigh, Sir Walter. *The English Novel*, London, 1907, p. 250.

(94) Cross, W.L. *The Development of the English Novel*, New York and London, 1930, p. 104.

(95) *A Bibliography...*, loc. cit.

lay unsold at a bookseller's, with only one or two discriminating readers to recognise its merit, as befell Landor's *Gebir* (1798) and Fitzgerald's *Omar Khayyam* (1838). It was rather the exceptional circumstances under which the book was first published that robbed the work of any such chance. These circumstances, like everything about the author of *Vathek,* were indeed unique. They have also rendered the book one of the exciting bibliographical problems of the nineteenth century.

Beckford had thought to make a mark in the world of letters with the tale in which "he dramatised his life in terms of the *Arabian Nights*". He had thought to achieve through literary fame the place in the front rows of society which he considered his right by birth, wealth and talents. He had started on the tale early in 1782 after the hectic Christmas festivities of 1781 in which he enjoyed the full liberty of his newly attained majority and engaged Zemir to serve oriental tales "hot", to satisfy the exotic tastes of the few "souls" invited to the strange party. The tale was composed in French and the Rev. Samuel Henley who had probably been present at the memorable festivities in the capacity of tutor to Beckford's Hamilton cousins, was engaged to translate the tale into English and compile the notes from Eastern writers. As the work proceeded the author's appreciation of his own creation grew considerably, and he started to compose a number of Episodes to accompany the tale of the Caliph and give the work a truly oriental form. The book was to appear first in French, in conformity with the major oriental tales of the century. Henley would then publish his English translation and the book would thus make its mark on the literary world, both sides of the Channel.

When Beckford was obliged to retire to Switzerland in 1785, because of the storm of the Powderham scandal, he clearly instructed Henley not to publish the translation for another year. He wrote to Henley in February 1786 :

> The publication of Vathek must be suspended at least another year. I would not have him on any account precede the French edition... The Episodes to Vathek are nearly finished, and the whole thing will be completed in eleven to twelve months... notwithstanding my eagerness to see

Vathek in print, I cannot sacrifice the French edition to my impatience. The anticipation of so principal a tale as that of the Caliph would be tearing the proudest feather from my turban. (96)

When Beckford lost his wife a few months later, he thought that the publication of the book would be delayed indefinitely. Henley, however, had already published the book in the form described above. He concealed Beckford's authorship and sometimes went so far as to give presentation copies signed by him "with the compliments of the author". As G. Chapman rightly guesses, he was probably hard up for money and what is more, he must have felt secure in Beckford's situation which had driven such a mighty millionnaire to self-exile on the Continent. (There is a hint of blackmail in Henley's long winded reply to Beckford's solicitor, in an oblique allusion to "a late unhappy occurrence". (97)

All that Beckford could do under those circumstances, was to set his solicitor at the publisher. He wrested the balance of the edition before it had had any chance to be widely bought or known. Consequently, copies of the first edition of *Vathek* must have become very rare, for Beckford could not leave the book in the market and write to any of the English *Journals*, declaring his authorship. It was less than two years since his name had been mongered in the press in connection with the Powderham scandal. Only a month or two before, some of the most forward in their war on the now unpopular millionnaire had returned to the attack. The occasion was the death of his young wife who, they alleged, had died of a broken heart, after suffering terrible illtreatment from her husband. The ambitious author was thus hedged in. All he could do was issue a French edition as soon as possible.

The first French edition of *Vathek* was published in Lausanne, 1787. Beckford briefly stated his authorship and disclaimed any connection between *Vathek* and the oriental manuscripts to which Henley had referred in his preface:

---

(96) *The Episodes of Vathek...* ed. cit., pp. XXX-XXII.
(97) *Ibid.*, p. XXV.

> L'ouvrage que nous présentons au public a été composé, en François, par M. Beckford. L'indiscrétion d'un homme de Lettre à qui le manuscrit avoit été confie, il y a trois ans, en a fait connoître la traduction angloise avant la publication de l'original. Le Traducteur a même pris sur lui d'avancer, dans sa Préface, que Vathek était traduit de l'Arabe. L'Auteur s'inscrit en faux contre cette assertion, et, s'engage à ne point en imposer au public sur d'autres ouvrages de ce genre qu'il se propose de faire connoître, il les puisera dans la collection précieuse de manuscrits orientaux laissés par... M. Worthley Montague, et dont les originaux se trouvent à Londres chez M. Palmer, Régisseur du Duc de Bedford. (98).

The edition had clearly been prepared in a great hurry, and the copious notes were dispensed with, except for very brief explanations of only four terms, "Goule", "Ginn", "Peris" and "Giaour". (99)

To add to the enigmas attending the publication of *Vathek* another French edition appeared in Paris in the same year. (100). Beckford's name was not mentioned in this edition. Some sixty-nine notes translated from those compiled by Henley were included in an abridged form. This text was obviously authorized by the author for it was used in later editions, though it retained many mistakes: Sale was often written Salé, Koran was written Horan and Al-Sirat turned into Al-Siral.

The problem of the two French editions published in the same year has been one of the numerous riddles which have puzzled bibliographers to the present time. Th encroachment of the Paris publisher on the rights of the publisher of Lausanne and the difference which ensued seem to have made the book very little known even in France. Some ninety years later, Stephane Mallarmé introducing a new edition of *Vathek*, 1876, (101) asserted that the two editions were apparently not

---

(98) *Vathek*, A Lausanne, chez Isaac Hignou et Comp., 1787, pp. III-IV.
(99) *Ibid.*, 204.
(100) *Vathek, Conte Arabe*, A Paris, chez Poincot... 1787.
(101) Beckford, William. *Le Vathek de Beckford, Reimprimé sur l'Edition française originale, avec Préface par Stephane Mallarmé,* Paris, Adolphe Labitte, 1876.

The edition used was the Paris edition, 1787 and the mistakes mentioned above were retained.

known at all. No mention of them was made in the literary circles of the period. Mallarmé himself had never heard of the book until Prosper Merimée drew his attention to it. ([102])

It is not surprising under these circumstances to find that *Vathek* had no impact on the oriental tale for many years after its publication in 1786. It was partly the author's fault that the book was so little known for more than twenty-five years. Even the publication of the 1809 edition was done very quietly and seems to have attracted little or no attention. While Beckford brooded over his *Episodes,* perfected his travel diaries or pursued his vain attempts to be presented at foreign courts or gain the peerage he was to have been awarded in 1784, writers without the least literary talent were publishing extremely bad translations from Arabic or Persian originals, and others without the least knowledge of either language were still publishing most glaring imitations. At a time when the wide demand in the book market allowed the publication of most trifling translations. Beckford had among his papers besides *Vathek,* a large number of translations and imitations from the *Arabian Nights* which he could have published if he had still been interested. *Vathek* remained, however, the only work of this type he published during his life.

## THE STORY OF AL RAOUI :—

The *Story of Al-Raoui* (1799) ([103]) generally ascribed to Beckford on the authority of Cyrus Redding ([104]), is now believed by some writers to have been published by Samuel Henley. The

---

(102) Parreaux, André, "Le Tombeau de Beckford par Stephan Mallarmé", *Revue d'Histoire Littéraire de la France,* Septembre 1955, 329-338.

(103) *The Story of Al Raoui, A Tale from the Arabic,* London, printed for Geisweiller, Pall Mall, 1799. In the *Catalogue of the British Museum,* the book is still catalogued under Beckford's name.

(104) The whole story of *Al Raoui,* together with dedication, Preface and accompanying verses are printed in Redding's *Memoirs.* He also states that the verses printed in the same volume were published in either *The Gentleman's Magazine* or *The Universal Magazine* between 1775- 1780. At that time Beckford could hardly have been engaged in composing pastorals on "Conjugal Love" and similar subjects. Redding, *op.cit.,* vol. I., 213 et seq.

story itself was a translation from the E.W. Montagu MSS. It is the same tale as that in Jonathan Scott's edition of the *Arabian Nights* (1811), called "Adventure of a Courtier, related by himself to his patron an Ameer of Egypt". [105]

The tale had appeared in Ouseley *Oriental Collections*, 1798, as a "Story from the Arabian Nights Literally translated by Jonathan Scott Esq" [106]. This had apparently induced Henley who was, a subscriber to the periodical [107], to publish the translation in his possession. He knew very well that both translations were from the same manuscript, but in one of his attempts to draw attention to himself, he did not say so directly in the preface to *Al Raoui*. He only said that the tale was one of the collection of tales mentioned in the preface to *The History of the Caliph Vathek*, that it had been ranslated sixteen years before and would not have been published,

> :but for notices of a manuscript possessed by Captain Scott which occur in Major Ouseley's curious Collections... The contents of a tale as there expressed suggest its identity or at least near similarity to this one...

There is a dedication to a certain Mrs. Cuthbert running.

> If this story of the Emir's an adept in his art, can afford you any amusement, it will be highly gratifying to the Translator.

It was very puzzling when viewed as published by Beckford. A German translation of the same tale and some verses were included in the slender volume (about sixteen pages in all). M.P. Conant mentioned the book in a brief note:

> Beckford also wrote a short oriental tale, *Al Raoui*, nominally "translated from the Arabic", but probably composed by Beckford, 1783, and first printed in 1799. It is a

---

(105) *The Arabian Nights' Entertainments, Carefully Revised and occasionally Corrected from the Arabic...*, by Jonathan Scott, in six vols., London, Longmans, 1811, VI, 229-237.

(106) *Oriental Collections*, 1798, 348-367.

(107) Henley had the year before contributed an article to the *Oriental Collections* in the form of a letter to the editor, explaining a Phœnician inscription in Wales, *Oriental Collections*, 1797, 337 ff.

fanciful and rather pleasing romantic tale and may be found in Cyrus Redding (¹⁰⁸)...

Conant, who has the *Oriental Collections* in her bibliography does not, however, seem to have examined them very carefully or she would not have doubted the authenticity of *Al Raoui*. Victor Chauvin in his review of Conant's book, asserted that the Story of *Al Raoui* was truly a translation from the Arabic. He mentioned his *Bibliographie des Ouvrages Arabes*, etc... V, pp. 116-117 (¹⁰⁹), as authority but he did not cast any doubt on Beckford being the translator :

Dr. J.W. Oliver was the first to cast doubt on Beckford being the translator of *Al Raoui* in his *Life of William Beckford* (London, 1932). Oliver's grounds for doubt were first the dedication to Mrs. Cuthbert and second the poems accompanying the translation. No Mrs. Cuthbert could anywhere be discovered in Beckford's letters or papers nor in his possible acquaintances. No. III of the poems included in the small volume is stated in Nichol's *Illustrations of the Literary History of the Eighteenth Century* to have been written by Henley in the winter of 1780 (¹¹⁰).

Guy Chapman had included the *Story of Al Raoui* in the *Bibliography of William Beckford* .. (1930) and had given descriptions of two editions which he naturally compared to the story reported in Redding's *Memoirs*, (1859) (¹¹¹). Oliver's doubts apparently set him more on his guard and after some research, he disqualified his own previous statements on the subjects of *Al Raoui*. In a letter to *The Times Literary Supplement*, (31st October, 1936), he added four more points to those mentioned by Oliver, all tending to support Henley's authorship :

---

(108) Conant, M.P. *op.cit.*, p. 71, No. 4.
(109) Chauvin, Victor. (Review of Conant), *op.cit.*, p. 258.
(110) Oliver. J.W. *op. cit.*, pp. 380-84.
(111) Chapman, Guy. *A Bibliography of William Bekford*, pp. 53-4.

1. Henley's reference to the *Story of Al Raoui* in one of the notes to the first edition of *Vathek* (1786) ([112]).

2. On examining Jonathan Scott's catalogue in the Bodleian Library (Notitia Cod. MI. NOCT. S.C. 28010) Guy Chapman found on p. 19:

> Story related to an Ameer of Egypt by a Courtier of his own Adventures, Nights 483-91... The same is given by the Rev. Samuel Henley under the title of Al Raoui, and also published in Sir William Ouseley's 'Oriental Collections' ... and published by Geisweiler, Pall Mall, 1799 ([113]).

Two more pieces of evidence mentioned by Chapman are not as conclusive as the above but they certainly add weight to the conclusion that it was *not* Beckford's work: One is that the two manuscripts (fair copies) of *Al Raoui* among the Beckford Papers in the Hamilton Muniments, are neither of them in Beckford's hand-writing. They do not contain any revisions or corrections (all his life, Beckford went over his own writings, correcting, perfecting etc... and with his letters falsifying them). Guy Chapman could identify the English version as in the hand-writing of Mme de Starck ([114]) but could not identify the hand-writing of the French copy. A final point supplied by Chapman is that no copy of *Al Raoui* appears in the Beckford Library

---

([112]) At Nouronihar's invitation to Vathek's sultanas to refresh themselves in the bath after their fatiguing journey, while the slaves amused them with tales, Henley commented, "The great have with reason regarded TALES as the best antidote to care". He quoted the opening passage of *Al Raoui* to illustrate the statement and mentioned that it was "Translated from one of the unpublished manuscripts mentioned in the preface", *An Arabian Tale* etc... (1786), p. 279. This, besides enhancing the illusion that *Vathek* itself was a translation of one of those manuscripts, was also probably an advertisement in advance for a publication of *Al Raoui* and other tales in some near future.

([113]) *The Times Literary Supplement* (31st October, 1936), p. 887.

([114]) Mme de Starck (1720-1804), "a writer of a little talent and a not incapable Orientalist", was a guest at Fonthill for Christmas 1782. Henley also was there and both he and Beckford were working on the E.W. Montagu manuscripts and on *Vathek*.

Sale of 1882-84, whereas all his other works figure in that sale.([115]).

The establishment of *Al Raoui* (1799), as the work of Samuel Henley would add to the little clergyman's credit without in the least detracting from Beckford's literary fame. On the contrary, the publication has always seemed too trifling for the author of *Vathek*. It has also seemed puzzling (to the present writer at least), why Beckford should have chosen this particular tale for publication in 1799, when he had the *Episodes*, the other translations from the *Arabian Nights* and the almost forgotten Caliph himself at his disposal. The reference to Jonathan Scott's translation published in the *Oriental Collections* did not seem a sufficient pretext, in my opinion. If Beckford had wished to compete with Jonathan Scott, (a thing he would not dream of; so vulgar and petty was Captain Scott by Beckford's standards !), he might have published the rest of his translations as the said Scott had declared his intention of publishing the whole translation of the *Arabian Nights*. On the other hand, ascribing the verses included in the volume to Henley, relieves Beckford's reputation from the dark shadow — which the shepherds and shepherdesses, Celias and Delias in the Poems reflected on his taste in poetry. One does not regard his impatience with Byron's verse in the same light as before. One can see in his exclamation at the fourth Canto of *Childe Harold*,

Words, words, words as loud as the sea and as empty !,

the refined taste of an artist of great economy of expression and not merely the jealous scoffing of an inferior poet.

The problem of its authorship apart, *The Story of Al Raoui* is itself too insignificant to change the fact that we are left with *Vathek* as Beckford's main contribution to the oriental tale, published during his life. This returns us to our original thesis that : after the abortive publication and near suppression of the only oriental tale composed in imitation of the *Arabian Nights* by an Englishman, that has stood the test of time, the author, for over wenty years, did not or could not make his book more ge-

---

(115) Cf. *infra*, for B. Alexander's replies to these objections.

nerally known to the world. Even when a new edition (or more probably the remainder of the first one with alterations in the name of the publisher on the title page) was published in 1809, no one took much trouble to make that much known either. *Vathek* might easily have been forgotten, if it had not by some lucky chance caught the imagination of a young but rising star.

## BYRON AND *VATHEK*:

It was Byron who first gave *Vathek* great publicity in a note to his successful Turkish tale, *The Giaour* (1813). He wrote as final note to his own tale :

> For the contents of some of the notes I am indebted partly to D'Herbelot, and partly to that most Eastern, and, as Mr. Weber justly entitles it, 'sublime Tale', the Caliph Vathek. I do not know from what source the author of that singular volume may have drawn his materials ; some of his incidents are to be found in the *Bibliothèque Orientale;* but for correctness of costume, beauty of description, and power of imagination, it far surpasses all European imitations and bears such marks of originality that those who have visited the East will find some difficulty in believing it to be more than a translation. As an Eastern tale, even *Rasselas* must bow before it ; his "Happy Valley" will not bear a comparison with the "Hall of Eblis" ([116]).

Byron's growing fame must have rendered *Vathek* a great service but Beckford did not appreciate the tribute of the young star. His publishers would print the famous "note" on the title-page of every new edition of *Vathek*, and though he often protested, he generally let it pass.

One can understand the older man's jealously of the fame Byron acquired with his Giaours and Corsairs. He considered himself a far superior author and speaking of the *Episodes* he asserted that if they ever saw the light, they would put Byron's Giaours into the shade. Byron too seems to have acquiesed into a feeling of Beckford's superiority and often sought to make his acquaintance or obtain a glimpse of his *Episodes,* but the millionnaire courteously refused. One suspects that Beckford

---

(116) Byron, *Poetry* III, 145.

knew full well that Byron's indebtedness to *Vathek* was much larger than the famous poet generally admitted.

This debt has been amply studied by many writers. One instance which Byron himself often mentioned, on the numerous occasions when he expressed his admiration for *Vathek*, was a passage in his *Siege of Corinth* (1816) ([117]). Years later, he told Medwin, his self-appointed Boswell:

> "Vathek" is another of the tales I had a very early admiration of. You may remember a passage I borrowed from it in 'The Siege of Corinth', which I almost took verbatim. No French man will believe that 'Vathek' is the work of a foreigner. It was written at seventeen (sic!). What do you think of the Cave of Eblis and the picture of Eblis himself? There is poetry... ([118])

M.P. Conant cited a few more examples of Byron's use of *Vathek* in his own works ([119]) but the debt was more thoroughly examined by Harold S.L. Wiener in 1938 ([120]). In his study of *The Giaour* (1813) in relation to *Vathek*, Wiener follows closely the annotations of E.H. Coleridge's edition of Byron's *Poetry* 1900. In fact the essential merit is that of Byron's editor. He examines the parallels between Byron's notes to *The Giaour* and Henley's

---

(117) The passage often cited is,
   There is a light cloud by the moon,
   'Tis passing, and will pass full soon
   If, by the time its vapoury sail Hath ceased her shaded orb to veil,
   Thy heart within thee is not changed;
   Dark will thy doom be, darker still
   Thine immortality of ill.

(Byron, *Poetry*, III, 478). The passage as Byron himself admitted was borrowed from the scene in which Providence attempts to save Vathek even on the brink of his ruin.

(118) Medwin, Thomas. *Conversations of Lord Byron*, London, 1824, pp. 237-8.

(119) Conant, M.P. *op.cit.*, Appendix A, 358-9.

(120) Wiener, Harold S.L. *The Eastern Background of Byron's 'Turkish Tales'*, Unpublished Doctoral Dissertation, Yale University, 1938. Part of the work was later published as "Byron and the East: Literary Sources of the 'Turkish Tales'", *Nineteenth Century Studies*, Ithaca, New York, Cornell University Press, 1940, 89-129. All references to Wiener are to this last work.

notes to *Vathek,* indicated by the same editor and adds some more parallels of his own like :

'Tis he ! the accursed Giaour !

in Byron's text. Those echoes of *Vathek,* however, might have come naturally to the poet after careful reading of Beckford's tale. Concerning the note to *The Giaour* quoted above, Wiener comes to the conclusion that :

> Byron's statement — that he was indebted to *Vathek* for the contents of some of his notes is.... but part of the truth. It may be seen that he used Henley's notes in the preparation of notes for his poem ; that he used Henley's notes in writing the poem itself ; that he used Beckford's story in the preparation of his own notes ; and that he used Beckford's story in the composition of his own poem. His indebtedness to *Vathek* is greater than he suggests in the note to the *Giaour* ([121]).

Wiener found many reminiscences of *Vathek* in Byron's second Turkish Tale, *The Bride of Abydos* (1813). The most striking is the close resemblance between Selim Byron's hero and Nouronihar's cousin Gulchenrouz. He found it logical to assume that Byron was still under the influence of *Vathek* when he composed the *Bride of Abydos* in November 1813. (*The Giaour,* "that snake of a poem which kept adding to its rattles" was composed in fragments between May and November, 1813. *The Bride,* according to Byron's *Journal,* was written in four nights in November, 1813).

By the time he wrote *The Corsair* (1814), the influence of *Vathek* had begun to wane, as direct connection with Beckford's book had ceased, reappearing once more in that passage of the *Siege of Corinth* (1816) ([122]).

Seventeen years later, André Parreaux covered the same

---

[121] *Ibid.,* 101.
[122] *Ibid.,* 103.

ground (¹²³), apparently, he was not aware of Wiener's work (¹²⁴) (which is not very easily available). Though he drew the same parallels as regards *The Giaour* and *The Bride of Abydos* as Wiener, the French writer does not stop at the *Turkish Tales*. He finds remininscences of *Vathek* in the fifth Canto of *Don Juan* and demonstrates clearly the influence of *Vathek* in *Manfred*. In fact, Parreaux's study leaves us nothing to add on Beckford and Byron. The influence, the parallels and contrasts not only of their works, but of their personal careers and social excommunication have been almost exhausted in this admirable paper (¹²⁵). The reader ends with a concrete picture of the magnitude of the influence of *Vathek*, not only "on Byron's youthful work" as Conant thought, but on all his work.

## VATHEK and MEJNOUN (1799) :-

Byron's use of Henley's notes had been anticipated, thirteen years earlier, by Isaac D'Israeli in *Mejnoun and Leila* (1799).(¹²⁶) This work was based on the abridged romance, published by the French orientalist Denis Cardonne in the *Bibliothèque Universelle des Romans* (April, 1778). I. D'Israeli's preface explained how the idea of the work was first suggested to him by an

---

(123) Parreaux, André, "Beckford et Byron", *Etudes Anglaises*, VIII (1955), 11-31 and 113-132.

(124) Wiener is not cited in Parreaux's notes,, which on the whole are quite exhaustive. In one context he remarks,
"Personne ne semble avoir remarqué, par exemple, que l'exclamation '...accursed Giaour' est sans doute un écho de *Vathek*", *ibid.*, 16
It is unnecessary to add that Wiener did notice the same echo seventeen years earlier.

(125) As this is a recent publication easily available, I have thought it unnecessary to go over the same ground in detail.

(126) D'Israeli, Isaac. *Mejnoun and Leila, The Arabian Petrarch and Laura*, in *Romances*, London, 1799, pp. 1-138.
— A 2nd edition of *Romances* was published London, 1801 (with the addition of a *Modern Romance*).
— *Mejnoun and Leila* was printed separately at Calcutta, n.d. (probably 1800).

illuminated Persian manuscript in the possession of the antiquary Francis Douce. The orientalist Sir William Ouseley had also shown him Sir William Jones's edition of a Persian poem by Hatefy on the same subject. Jones's English introduction to the Persian text had convinced D'Israeli of the importance and popularity of the story.

In his attempt to amplify the details of 'local colour', D'Israeli fell back on travel literature and on the notes of *Vathek*. He drew extensively on some of the longer specimens of Henley's erudition ([127]). He was obviously unaware of any distinction between the author of the book and the editor of the notes. ([128])

*VATHEK* and *SAFIE* (1814) :-

Byron's use of Henley's notes and Beckford's text was copied at a smaller scale by John Hamilton Reynolds in *Safie* (1814) ([129]). Henley's notes in particular, made a remarkable collection of oriental stuff, easily accessible to writers who were not in the habit of reading widely for their poems.

J.H. Reynolds did not mention the *Caliph Vathek* or its notes in his notes to *Safie* but it is quite clear that he had made use of them for compiling most of the twenty-eight notes appended to his *Eastern Tale*. Most of the notes were even taken verbatim from the notes of *Vathek* (1786), a thing which Byron (to whom the tale was dedicated) would never have done, at least without acknowledgement. One or two examples will be sufficient here :

Note 16 of *Safie* runs :

> The tulip a flower of Eastern growth, and there held in great estimation :-

Thus in an ode of Mesihi :

---

(127) e.g. Henley's long note on tinging the eyes of women (*An Arabian Tale*, 235) is quoted verbatim, *Romances* (1801), 123-4.
(128) "The author of the Caliph Vathek in his learned and agreeable notes..." *Romances* (1801), p. 119 and again, 121.
(129) Reynolds, J.H. *Safie, An Eastern Tale*, London, 1814.

> The edge of the bower is filled with the light of Ahmed; among the plants, the fortunate *Tulips* represent his companions ([130]).

This was copied word by word from a note by Henley ([131]) and shows that Reynolds had a copy of the first or second edition of *Vathek* before him, when he was writing his notes and did not only depend on recollection. How he expected his numerous borrowings to escape reviewers (of whom he was in mortal fright) ([132]), unless he was sure that no one but himself knew the work from which he borrowed so lavishly, I do not know ([133]).

A few more instances can be clearly seen in note 27, p. 90 of *Safie* ([134]), note 21, p. 88 ([135]), and note 14, p. 86 ([136]), which are mentioned merely as examples for I have traced every note of this *Eastern Tale* (1814) to one or two of the notes of Henley.

\* \* \*

## THE CALIPH AND HIS SUCCESSORS :-

*Vathek* was the product of a heated and highly sensitive imagination, long impregnated with the reading of the *Arabian Nights*, the *Persian Tales*, the works of early travellers to the East and probably Sir William Jones's impassioned dissertations in praise of Asiatic literature. The result was a work of great imagination, little known to the majority of readers at first, but of great impact on the verse tales of the Romantics. Southey read it when he was working on his *Arabian Tale, Thalaba* (1801) ([137]),

---

(130) *Ibid.*, 87.

(131) *An Arabian Tale...* (1786), 241-2

(132) See Byron's *Letters and Journals*, II, 288. Byron had to write to Francis Hodgson about the frightened poet and recommend that he be taken gently, *Lettetrs and Journals*, III, 51-2.

(133) This is hardly probable. *Safie* was dedicated to Byron and it is clear that it was written in imitation of his Turkish tale *The Giaour* (1813) in which Byron, as it were proclaimed the merits of *Vathek* from the housetops.

(134) Cf. *Arabian Tale*, 250.

(135) Cf. *Arabian Tale*, 229 and 233.

(136) Cf. *Arabian Tale*, 244.

(137) Southey, Robert. *Commonplace Book*, London, 1849-51, 4th series, 185.

though he did not refer to *Vathek* in his copious notes, owing probably, to the compromising character of the author. Byron was greatly influenced by it and was responsible for bringing it to the notice of the reading public in general. Thomas Moore utilised the romantic picture of the East it evoked : the land of horrid precipices and fertile valleys, where Nouronihar ran, her hair floating in the breeze, throwing jessamines at the enraptured Caliph and where he later wandered in frenzied despair at the supposed death of his beloved, was indeed a suitable background for the romantic tales which Feramorz sang to the young royal bride in *Lalla Rookh* (1817). His Gueber rebel scaled impossible towers to penetrate to the chamber of Hinda, daughter of his Arabian oppressor. His heroines raved in madness at the loss of love or honour, and one of his heroes, Azim, spent the remainder of his life a hermit, watering the grass and flowers that grew near his Zelica's grave. This colourful but shaky edifice which Beckford had conjured out of his imagination and travellers' lore, and to which Byron contributed in spite of his having been "on the spot", remained the stock background of the oriental tale until it was shattered to pieces by works like Thomas Hope's *Anastasius* (1818) and James Justinian Morier's *Hajji Baba* (1824).

On the other hand, the oriental tale in prose went on its course (as described by Conant) for the most part undisturbed by the presence of Beckford's work among its ranks. By the time the book attained its long delayed popularity (owing to the publicity which accompanied the sale of Fonthill Abbey in 1822) ([138]), new factors had appeared on the scene, which made it impossible for the Caliph to exercise any wide influence in this field. Political events ([139]) were drawing the "glorious for off

---

(138) It was then that "any sense or nonsense connected with Fonthill sold like wild-fire". The 1816 edition was presumbly sold out and a new edition was published ni 1823. In 1834 it was included in Bentley's cheap edition of *Standard Novels*.

(139) The establishment of the British empire in India, the French Expedition to Egypt (1797-1800), British interference for the evacuation of the French, the growth of commerce with India and other countries of the East and finally the Allied war against Mohammed Ali in Syria were all contributing factors.

East" much nearer to Europe than it had ever been. It was now overrun by merchants, soldiers and diplomats of the Great Powers, competing at that time for establishing the priority of their interests in the East (Britain, France and Russia).

The ancient sacred languages of the East had been "forced" one after another. English scholars in India had started to learn Sanskrit as early as 1785, and had generously taught it to scholars of other European nationalities.

Other languages soon followed : ancient Pehlevi in 1793, the Cuneiform in 1803, Hieroglyphics in 1822 and Zend in 1832([140]). Though achievements in this field opened before the eyes of historians and archaelogists vistas of splendid ancient civilizations, in many cases superior even to the glory that was Greece or Rome, those realms of gold were not for the common traveller or the ordinary man of letters ; they passed into the strictly scientific field of the specialist. The ruins of Persepolis, Memphis or Palmyra passed from the wondering gaze of a Chardin or a Volney to the cold scrutiny of specialists who would one day decipher the mystic characters on the walls and read the history of ancient monarchs and other "creatures of clay" who had once inhabited these splendid palaces, wrought by the artifice of clever craftsmen who were, nevertheless, ordinary men "who ate onions for their labour !"

The study of the classics of Eastern nations had also passed into the sequestered domain of specialisation. Romantic encyclopaedic works like D'Herbelot's *Bibliothèque Orientale*, Richardson's *Dissertation* (1777) and Jones's numerous essays on the *Literature of Asiatic Nations* (1771-3), which had inspired the young author of *Vathek* had been replaced by the learned productions of Asiatic Societies and the Oriental Translation Fund ([141]). The enthusiastic, imaginative but sweeping generalisations of Jones or Richardson were giving way to the dry

---

(140) For a detailed account see Schwab, Raymond. *La Renaissance Orientale*, Payot, Paris, 1950.

(141) The Asiatic Society of Bengal was founded in Calcutta by Sir William Jones early in 1784. The French Asiatic Society was founded in Paris, 1822. The Royal Asiatic Society of Great Britain, in London, 1824 and the Oriental Translation Fund was engrafted upon it in 1828. **Membership was open** to scholars particularly orientalists of all nationalities.

scientific exactitude of Colebrooke or Hodgson. The orientalist ceased to address himself to men of letters in general and restricted himself to the narrow circle of equally specialised scholars, who were best qualified to appreciate his work.

The traveller, on the other hand, whether soldier, diplomat or leisured "globe-trotter", still continued to address the reading public in general ([142]). Though obliged to discard his original vocation of adding "to the stock of human knowledge", he could still impart information on "manners and customs" and henceforth focussed his attention on the contemporary scene which, to say the truth, was far from flattering. A traveller with a dash of poetry could in 1819 still dwell on the romantic possibilities of such travel ([143]) but others like James Justinian Morier were laying the inscrutable East open before the eyes of their countrymen. The poverty, the ignorance and the decay underlying the magnificent edifice of wealth and splendour with which Oriental despots were surrounded, from the Persian Shah or the Turkish Sultan to their numerous walis and deputies were all exposed by the penetrating pen of the traveller. The diplomatic rivalry between Britain and France revealed the corruption of ministers, who could be bribed to do anything, but were nevertheless abject slaves of the Monarch whose word was law. A little knowledge of the language as a result of a few years' residence revealed also the decay of literature, the ignorance of professedly learned men and the stupidity of court poets eking out a livelihood by fawning praise on the reigning monarchs and attributing to them virtues they never possessed.

---

(142) For a detailed account see :

Brown, Wallace Cable. "The Popularity of English Travel Books about the NEAR EAST, 1775-1825", *Philological Quartely*, XV, (1936), 70-80.

and Anis, Mohammed. "British Travellers' Impressions of Egypt in the Late Eighteenth Century", *Bulletin of the Faculty of Arts, Fouad I University*, Cairo. XIII, pt II (December, 1951), pp. I ff.

and Rushdy, Mohammad Rashad. "English Travellers in Egypt During the Reign of Mohammed Ali" *Bulletin of the Faculty of Arts, Fouad I Univ.*, Cairo, XIV, pt II (Dec 1952), 1-61.

(143) Henry Gally Knight, one of Byron's imitators wrote in 1819, "...in touching upon the countries of the East, truth and poetry may still be united ...romantic adventures are daily occurences", *Eastern Sketches* 2nd ed., London, 1819, pp. vii-viii.

The traveller, who had lost so many grounds to the specialist, now claimed the oriental tale as his special domain and after the publication of Morier's *Hajji Baba of Ispahan* (1824), it was ceded to him without contest. In 1834 (the year *Vathek* was included in Bentley's *Standard Novels*), Morier dedicated a new oriental romance *Ayesha, The Maid of Kars* to the "Travellers in the East, whom the author (one of themselves) considered the best judges of his book", but the fact was almost established by then. Sir Walter Scott had recognised it as early as 1825 when, harassed by debts and pressed for new material by the horde of imitators who were always close at his heels, he would not listen to friends urging him to try his hand at an oriental tale, a surely profitable literary enterprise at the time. He turned to the Crusades instead, and to his favourite hero Richard the Lion-heart when he wrote *The Talisman* (1825).

His preface to the edition of 1832 shows that he deliberately abstained from dabbling with what he regarded as the traveller's domain:

> I felt the difficulty of giving a vivid picture of a part of the world with which I was almost totally unacquainted, unless by early recollections of the "Arabian Night Enterainments"; and not only did I labour under the incapacity of ignorance,... but my contemporaries were, many of them, as much enlightened upon the subject as if they had been inhabitants of the favoured land of Goshen. The love of travelling had pervaded all ranks, and carried the subjects of Britain into all quarters of the world... Had I, therefore, attempted the difficult task of substituting manners of my own invention, instead of the genuine costume of the East, almost every traveller I met, who had extended his route beyond what was anciently called "The Grand Tour", had acquired a right, by ocular inspection, to chastise me for my presumption... It occurred, therefore, that where the author of *Anastasius*, as well as he of *Hajji Baba*, had described the manners and vices of the Eastern nations, not only with fidelity, but with the humour of Le Sage and the ludicrous power of Fielding himself, one who was a perfect stranger to the subject must necessarily produce an unfavourable contrast ([144]).

---

(144) Scott, Sir Walter. *Works...*, With all his *Introductions and Notes*, IV, Edinburgh, 1851, p. 587.

And what became of the oriental tale in the hands of these travellers after the testimony of such an authority as Sir Walter Scott ? The shaky edifice of a romantic East raised by Beckford and exploited to a nauseating extent by Byron, Moore and their imitators was undermined by the publications of these prosaic travellers who could boast a more detailed knowledge of one part or another of the falsely romanticised East. The details of information they had to impart were presented in a more imaginative form than the mere *Travel ;* they sent an imaginary Oriental (certainly not a Caliph but one of his meanest subjects) on the route they themselves had traversed and let his adventures speak for themselves. The most successful of their number was indeed the author of *Hajji Baba* (1824) who brought the hero of the oriental tale down from the summit of his tower of a thousand steps, where he had observed the stars and sacrificed to the powers of darkness. He left his Palace of the Five Senses, rich with the treasures of art and literature. He quitted the Hall of Subterranean Fire where he had wandered in sublime damnation. From the ruins of Istakhar, he walked the dirty narrow streets of Isfahan and sat in his father's shop close to a big caravanserai, shaving heads, trimming beards and cracking the joints of merchants and mule-drivers, discussing the "price of lamb's wool in Constantinople."

The change from highly-wrought romance to the palpable though ignoble contemporary reality of the streets of Isfahan, was, in some respects, a step forward. As an Indian writer has put it,

> ...at last, in 1824, a decisive blow was struck at all the false sentiment attaching to an East as little understood as visited, when James Justinian Morier launched upon the world his immortal hero,... Here at last was the oriental Gil Blas, naked and unashamed ([145]).

In him lay the hope of wresting the oriental tale from the misty pinnacles of romance and incorporating it in the growing realistic tradition of the English novel, if it were to survive at all in the age of the railway and the Exhibition.

---

(145) Dunn, T.O.D. "Meadows Taylor, his Autobiography and Novels," *The Calcutta Review*, N.S., VI (Jan., 1918), p. 27.

To conclude, though *Vathek* remained, as a literary curiosity and a precious bauble to be repeatedly reprinted and reread, the Caliph could boast of no worthy successor in the age of P & O steam service and Lieutenant Waghorn's well appointed four-horse Suez mail which carried ladies with reticules and lapdogs across the desert from Cairo to Suez, as regularly and as comfortably as they might be carried from London to Bath or Brighton.

Sir Walter Scott kept his Saladin strictly within the bounds of European traditions concerning the Crusades. Saladin had been the only hero among the Muslim combatants to be appropriated by European legends. In the *Talisman* he is a thorough-bred knight, wiser indeed and more chivalrous than many of the crusading princes who could boast no peer to the Oriental potentate in their ranks but the English Lion-heart and the poor Scottish Knight, (heir to the Scottish throne *incognito*).

Thomas Moore's *Epicurian* (1827) can hardly be affiliated to *Vathek*. The material included was Christian, Classical and Ancient Egyptian. Though the *Memoirs* of the author show that the process of collecting material extended over a period of seven years (1820-1827) and included visits to the Egyptian Institute in Paris and conversations with French artists and *savants* who had accompanied Napoleon's Expedition to Egypt in 1797 ([146]), the tale was the worst of Moore's excursions into fields of which he was originally ignorant. Owing to its Christian proselytism, the *Epicurean* found many admirers who wrote "flaming eulogies" in the press which the author proudly recorded in his diary. It realised 700 pounds in royalties ([147]) but was met by scathing criticism from true scholars among men of letters like T.L. Peacock who dismissed the display of learning made in the numerous notes (modelled on Henley's notes to *Vathek*) as,

---

([146]) Moore, Thomas. *Memoirs, Journal and Correspondence*, ed. Lord John Russell, London, 1860, pp. 263-8.

([147]) At least four editions of the *Epicurean* were published by Longman's London in 1827. An English edition was published in Paris, 1827, another one 1828. A French translation was published Paris, 1827, a German translation Innsbruch, 1828 and a Spanish, Barcelona, 1832 (!).

> ...small scraps of many authors, raked together, manifestly, not by reading but by dipping, and making a display very nearly equivalent, both in manner and matter, to the series of learned labels on an apothecary's empty boxes. (148)

In 1833, a young foppish admirer of Beckford, just back from a tour of the Near East, published *Alroy* in which he drew largely on *Vathek*. Benjamin Disraeli's romance is fantastically inferior when compared to the original model. The supernatural machinary which enables the hero to gain the Sceptre of Solomon rather smacks of the hocus pocus. of a shabby juggler. The princess Schirine the Caliph's daughter, modelled on Beckford's Nouronihar, is a fastidious, spoilt, English coquette, with a gazelle on a gold chain in place of a dog !

Beckford was proud of the young author's tribute and expressed his admiration for *Alroy* in rather exaggerated terms,

> ...most proud I am to perceive that he is so strongly imbued with *Vathek* — the images it presents haunt him continually — the halls of Eblis, the thrones of the Sulimans are for ever present to his mind's eye, tinted with somewhat different hues from those of the original, but partaking of the same awful and dire solemnity (149).

In the bitterness of his own disappointed isolation, the old man knew well enough that *Alroy* had little or no chance of success :

> I doubt, however that it will take, or that... [it] can be appreciated by the gross rattling readers of the present cold hearted period (150).

After another stretch of years we get Meredith's *Shaving of Shagpat* (1855). Though modelled on the *Arabian Night* and showing clear traces of the influence of *Vathek*, Meredith's fantastic oriental tale is so fraught with the insinuanting presence of that lying, scheming barber from Isfahan who stepped into the oriental tale in 1824, that the dignity of the Caliph's quest is turned into a laughing stock.

---

(148) *The Westminster Review*, VIII (1827), p. 384.
(149) Oliver, J.W. *op.cit.*, p. 300.
(150) *Ibid.*, 297-8.

# PSEUDO-ORIENTALISM IN TRANSITION: THE AGE OF *VATHEK*

*By*

MAHMOUD MANZALAOUI

The main contribution in the celebration of this, the Beckford bi-centenary year, is undoubtedly Monsieur André Parreaux' huge volume *William Beckford: Auteur de 'Vathek'*.([1]) One of the most interesting of the more general discussions in the book is in that section of Chapter VI (*'Vathek' et le conte oriental au XVIIIe siècle)* entitled 'L'heure de Vathek' : an attempt at describing the precise climate of pseudo-oriental and imaginative 'orientalizing' literature around the year 1783. Monsieur Parreaux distinguishes some of the developments which mark the closing years of the century as being somewhat different in attitude from the earlier decades, and also distinguishes, as Miss Conant has already done, ([2]) between the age of the pseudo-oriental prose tale, and the Romantic period which was to succeed.

The purpose of this essay is to provide an extension of Monsieur Parreaux' study of the last quarter of the eighteenth-century as a pivotal phase in 'pseudo-orientalism', and thus emphasize the special status that may be accorded to *Vathek*. It also points to a further distinction not made by Miss Conant and Monsieur Parreaux, between the Romantic phase which followed, and the more realistic phase which was to follow upon that.

Miss Conant's division of the oriental tale of the eighteenth century into four categories has been found useful by all students of the minor literature of England and France in that

---

(1) Paris, 1960.
(2) Martha P. Conant, *The Oriental Tale in England in the Eighteenth Century*, New York, 1908.

period. The 'moralistic', 'philosophical', and 'satirical' groups are well-defined, and typical of the age. From certain points of view, however, the grouping of the more creative and adventurous experiments under the heading 'imaginative' is unsatisfactory. One has to guard against a tendency to think that none of the moral, philosophical or satirical tales have any imaginative qualities, and against a tendency to neglect the very considerable differences in the 'imaginative' quality of different tales in this group. Above all, Miss Conant's treatment, which does not cover the Romantic period, come close to abolishing this extremely important phase of creative orientalism, or, at least, to squeezing it in tightly between eighteenth-century pseudo-orientalism, and modern, accurate, oriental studies.

She ends (pp. 255-6) with a reference to new forces already at work at the close of the century:

> 'the increased number of travellers' accounts and... the accompanying activity of orientalists... Direct translations from oriental languages into English made a notable contribution to English knowledge of Eastern life and literature, and had a large share in turning the imagination of nineteenth-century poets and story-tellers toward the use of oriental material. This chapter — still in the making — has been distinguished throughout its entire course by actual first-hand knowledge of the Orient, — one vital characteristic which throws it into sharp contrast with the chapter discussed in the present volume.'

This statement pays no attention to the fact that the scholarly translations of imaginative literature did not affect the body of non-specialist literature in the manner she describes until towards the middle of the nineteenth century. Even direct experience, such as Byron's travels, did not produce the 'true' orientalism which Miss Conant is alluding to — the oriental knowledge of Lane, Kinglake, and the Victorian scholar-traveller. In general, Monsieur Parreaux (pp. 332-4) adopts the same attitude as Miss Conant.

A truer picture of developments would, I think, see the first thirty years of the nineteenth century as a period which made its own particular imaginative use of orientalism, a poetic, personal, use, which is very different from the true orientalism of the Victorian Age. If any category of oriental fiction deserves the name 'imaginative' as a group, it is not the imitation of translated oriental tales in the eighteenth century, but the oriental verse tale of the age of Shelley, Byron, Moore, Landor, and Southey : a judgement with which, I think, from his remarks on p. 328, Monsieur Parreaux will agree. Compared to their use of oriental themes, Miss Conant's 'imaginative' group might more accurately be termed 'imitative', or, in the Coleridgean sense, 'fanciful.'

By over-emphasizing the 'imaginative' quality of eighteenth-century pseudo-oriental fantasies, by under-estimating the importance of the Romantic phase, by placing the mainstream of the influence of accurate orientalism too soon, Miss Conant's classification blurs an important distinction : the distinction between two phases of pseudo-orientalism, the fanciful, and the Romantic. Her terminology is out of focus because, on the whole, Miss Conant's study of the eighteenth-century is 'synchronous', and does not sufficiently reveal the evolution of eighteenth-century orientalism, from an imitation of the *Arabian Nights,* at the opening of the century, to a period of tentative exploration in the closing decades, and from that to the poetic orientalism of the 'semi-romantics'. Miss Conant's study thus particularly evades the issue of the modifications taking place in the final quarter of the century : and it has required Monsieur Parreaux' discussion (pp. 325-8) to make this evident.(³) At the other end of the period, in contrast, her discussion is extremely lucid : in her *Introduction,* she touches upon the continuity between the mediaeval tale of oriental wonders, and the treatment of similar themes in Renaissance drama, with the parallel transition from the latter, through the French pseudo-oriental novel of the seventeenth century, to the

---

(3) The distortion of view is, I think, partly due to the attempt to include Parnell's *Hermit* synchronically in a group which also includes *Rasselas* and *Vathek*. The *Hermit* is considerably earlier, is in verse, and is 'pseudo-oriental' is an entirely different sense, being an 'unorientalized' version of an oriental tale.

eighteenth-century tale. At the same time as she points to this measure of continuity, she rightly stresses that the appearance of the *Arabian Nights* provided a new point of departure : and, indeed, it is almost exclusively with imitations and derivatives of the *Nights* that her book deals.

To see *Vathek* against the background of the pseudo-orientalism of its generation is both to place it more exactly in its historical position, and to appreciate its value more greatly, as a work rising above the experimentation of Beckford's coevals, and, indeed, in some ways reacting sharply against them. The pages that follow are, therefore, intended to review some of the developments in pseudo-orientalism in England in the years from the appearance of Warton's *History of English Poetry* to immediately before the appearance of the oriental poems of the Romantics. I have included the study of genuine oriental features, when used, accurately or not, as part of general non-orientalist scholarship. I fear this may be taken to mean that I am extending the use of the term 'pseudo-oriental' to trends that cannot strictly be embraced by the term : my plea is that I am discussing all 'oblique' uses made of oriental matter, whether in the imaginative literature which has an eastern setting, or in the criticism and scholarship which seize upon a fragmentary knowledge of things eastern for purposes of their own. The conclusion that can be made from this, sometimes disjointed, survey are, in sum, and apart from the disagreement already stated, those of Monsieur Parreaux, reached from a slightly divergent point of departure.

The turn of the century saw the use of Arabic studies, and of their *matériel*, in fields of non-orientalist activity. The pseudo-orientalism of the preceding century, deriving mainly from the *Nights,* had set in its way, principally in the production of moral and satirical tales. Cazotte's *Suite des mille et une nuits* (1788) reinforced this trend, but new tendencies were already at work. A new shade of pseudo-orientalism colours the last quarter of the century : tentative uses are made of things oriental, uses which for the most part, are misdirected or feeble.

Orientalism is used by the writers of a new genre, children's literature; it is somewhat cavalierly appropriated by the new antiquarians and mediaevalists; the streamlet of pseudo-orientalism spreads out over the new-preoccupations of an experimental and transitional period. One experiment bore fruit: the 'moral' oriental tale was given a new dimension by the didactic 'immoralism' of Beckford, the 'fanciful' oriental tale was deepened by Beckford's use of it for fancies of a kind at once more deeply personal and more widely humane. *Vathek* is, in a sense, the culmination-point of the trends of oriental fiction which Miss Conant assesses; with *Rasselas* and *Vathek* written, these had achieved as much as they ever could. From another point of view *Vathek,* the last of the eighteenth-century prose tales, ushers in the verse tales of Byron, Moore, and Southey: the subjective inspiration, the love of exotic—and artificially enhanced—local colour, and the imaginative use of facts derived from academic sources such as encyclopaedias, three leading characteristics of this next phase—are established by Beckford.

The genuine orientalist studies of the time, (the age, indeed, of Sir William Jones) are considerable. A weakness of the orientalizing tendencies of the period is, however, their failure to integrate true orientalism with other spheres of scholarship, and, in addition, the failure to present a field of knowledge sufficiently well-attested (as, for example, could classical scholars) to prevent imaginative writers (including Beckford) from building up a literature based upon a self-centered and inaccurate use of the researches of scholars. This tendency did not start with the Romantics who in this, as in many other points, were continuing the tendencies of the latter part of the eighteenth century. *Pace* Monsieur Parreaux, in his note 14 on p. 172, one cannot help noting that Beckford, in spite of his proved knowledge of Arabic, is deeply influenced by pseudo-orientalism, yet innocent of any intellectual or verbal *calque* which might have pointed to direct Arabic influence upon his writing.

In that active period of scholarship, even the most distinguished orientalism is erratic by present standards. Of more interest to us here, however, are those activities of general scholarship which touched upon Arabic studies, but had a leaning towards some other alien interest or opinion, which resulted in a distortion of view. The scholarship of the time examined much that was new to those whose learning was in the tradition of the preceding generations. One might generalize, and point to two main new tendencies. One was to assimilate into the cultural background—classical in taste, neatly planned-out in its structure—the fresh and widely-varying interests which were developing. The second, was to break away from the traditional outlook, and point with enthusiasm to re-orientation and revaluation. One may call the notion of 'universal grammar'—defined by Harris and by Alexander Tytler,[4] an attempt at Assimilation, while Warton's *History* is a clarion call for Reorientation. The *Arabian Nights* and other Arabic works gained attention in both those tendencies.

The tradition into which the attempt to assimilate oriental literature yielded the most interesing results is that of classical studies. Two other non-orientalist spheres of accustomed literary activity incorporated Arabic fiction as a section of their interests, and these must first be mentioned. In the field of didactic fiction, from the early years of the eighteenth century, the tales of the *Arabian Nights* were quoted, adapted, and imitated. From Miss Conant we learn of the numerous moral, philosophical, and satirical works written in imitation of the *Nights*. Suited in form for use as apologues, the *Nights* nevertheless lose most of their original qualities when treated in this manner.

The second of these fields of activity is the academical work of the Church of England. In this period as in the seventeenth century, the interest arises as an ancillary to missionary work and to Biblical studies. Porteus, Bishop of London, '...often and seriously lamented, that oriental literature was not sufficiently cultivated by those who were destined for the ministerial

---

(4) George Harris, Hermes (1751), p.x., '... universal grammar ... that grammar, which without regarding the several idioms of particular languages, only respects those principles that are essential to them all'.

Alexander Fraser Tytler, *On the Principles of Translation*, (1791) p. 160, '... idioms, or terms of expression which do not belong to universal grammar.'

office in the church,' and, with this in mind, appointed to an English living a German who had lived in the East.(⁵) The preface to Ouseley's *Oriental Collections* (1797-1800), points out the usefulness of Arabic for theological and Biblical studies, and states that the periodical will deal with 'Hebraeo-Biblical' matters without indulging in theological controversy. The Prospectus for an intended publication, *Annals of Oriental Literature*, a copy of which was sent to Francis Douce,(⁶) calls Biblical criticism 'the most valuable branch of Oriental Learning'. In later years, such work appeared as *Oriental Literature applied to the Illustration of Holy Scripture*, by Samuel Burder (1807), and *Eastern Manners and Customs, Illustrative of Scripture*, published by Nelson (1857).(⁷) When one great field of scholarship is viewed as ancillary to another, rather different one, no profound or seminal work should be expected : it must be remembered, that, even so, a great deal of George Sale's orientalist work was carried out at the request of the Society for the Promotion of Christian Knowledge.

Turning now to the attempt to assimilate the *Arabian Nights* into the classical tradition which formed the cultural background of the time, we find that it is the Homeric parallels of the *Nights* which attracted most attention. Already Galland himself, writing to Huet on February 25th, 1701, had said of his tales, 'Il y en a deux qui semblent esté tirez d'Homère. En effet, l'on y reconnoît dans l'un la fable de Circé, et celle de Polyphème dans l'autre.' (⁸) There can be no doubt that the tales referred to are *Beder and Giauhare* and the *Third Voyage*

---

(5) William Beloe, *The Sexagenarian* (1817), pp. 431-4.
(6) The Prospectus is pasted into vol. ii of Douces's copy of Ouseley's *Collections*, now in the Bodleian.
(7) Similar publications are John Callaway's *Oriental Observations* (1827), Maria Hack's *Oriental Fragments* (1828), and Robert Jamieson's *Eastern manners, illustrative of the Old Testament* (1836).
(8) E. Zotenberg, *Notice sur quelques MS. des Mille et une Nuits et la traduction de Galland (Notices et extraits des MS. de la Bibliothèque Nationale. xxviii)*; Paris, 1887; p. 170.

of *Sindbad*. (⁹)  In Clara Reeve's *Progress of Romance* (1785), a critical essay in conversational form, are two passages in which the *Nights* are discussed. In the first of the two (i. 22 ff.) while the conversation turns open Homer, the subject of the *Nights* is introduced by Euphrasia.

> 'Euphrasia :  ...Did you never read a book called the Arabian Nights Entertainments ?
> Hortensius : You cannot be in earnest in this comparison ?'

Euphrasia proceeds to enumerate the points in which 'the Arabian writer' resembles Homer : the general characteristics of bold imagination, of their variety of characters, of their relating of marvellous adventures ; the more particular characteristic of 'Machinery'.  The 'Arabian' she finds the more modest of the two in his use of Machinery : Homer is constantly sending his deities on the most trifling errands, but the genii of the Arabian are all subordinate to the seal of Solomon. In conclusion, Euphrasia adds that 'it is likewise worthy of observation ; that throughout the whole work, the Supreme Being is never mentioned without the deepest marks of homage and veneration.' Hortensius is of opinion that the 'Arabian writer imitated Homer as many others have done' ; Euphrasia lays down that 'there is frequently a striking resemblance between works of high and low estimation, which prejudice only, hinders us from discerning, and which, when seen, we do not care to acknowledge.' This curious discussion ends with a summing-up which is, in effect, a more generalized restatement of the last two points :

> 'First that Epic Poetry is the parent of Romance. Secondly, That there is a certain degree of respect due to all the works of Genius, by whatever name distinguished.'

---

(9) Zotenberg does not appear to have noted that this remark almost certainly proves Galland  to have been in possession of a copy, not only of *Sindbad*, but of a collection which included *Beder and Giauhare*, as early at the date of this letter. In fact, he appears by then to have already transated both the tales mentioned.

## PSEUDO-ORIENTALISM IN TRANSITION : THE AGE OF *VATHEK*

Both the comparison with Homer, and the desire to vindicate the *Nights* against belittling criticism, are more fully developed in the first book devoted entirely to a study of the latter work : *Remarks on the Arabian Nights' Entertainments ; in which the Origin of Sindbad's Voyages, and the other Oriental Fictions, is particularly considered.* By Richard Hole, LL.B.... 1797. Hole,([10]) the author of an *Essay on the character of Ulysses, as delineated by Homer,* published posthumously ([11]), was also interested in mediaeval studies : in 1772 he published a poetic version of Macpherson's *Fingal,* and in 1789 appeared his poem *Arthur ; or the Northern enchantment,* based on the Arthurian legends. Already, in the *Preface* to the latter, he shows an interest in the *Arabian Nights* from the point of view of comparative literature. In a note, he expresses a wish that the work should be retranslated, and that it should no longer be considered as a children's book.([12]) Hole indicates those resemblances to the *Odyssey* upon which Galland has already commented, and adds points of comparison with Ariosto, Spenser, Chaucer, and Shakespeare.([13])

> 'From Circe originates the Alcina of Ariosto, and Acrasia of Spenser ; and, what is rather remarkable, each of them inserts a circumstance mentioned by the Arabian, but not noted in Homer, that of the metamorphosed gallants opposing the hero of the tale... Christopher Sly and the Nobleman, in Shakespeare's Induction to *Taming the Shrew* [sic], have their counterparts in *Abun-Hassan* [sic] and the Caliph Harun Al-rashid.' ([14])

Here, therefore, and to a greater extent in the *Remarks,* Hole makes numerous interesting and ingenious suggestions. However, the field remains an arid one, for he did not carry his interest so far as to learn the Arabic language, and acquire

---

(10) Bartholomew Parr, *A slight sketch of the life of the Rev. Richard Hole,* Exeter (1803) ; p. 3.
(11) In 1807.
(12) Hole, *Arthur,* p.v.
(13) *Ibid,* pp. v-vi.
(14) *Ibid,* p.vi., note.

the other qualifications necessary for any serious research. The fact that he knows no Arabic is clear from the general tenor of the *Remarks*, and the absence of any reference to Arabic works in the original; however, the footnote on his p. 146 and a passage quoted on p. 133 below, make it quite certain.

Hole's unfamiliarity with Arabic literature and its leading characteristics causes him to treat the *Nights* as a work of considerably higher standing than is actually the case. He knew nothing of the degenerate nature of the language and style, of the gap which divided this genre of literature from the main body of writing that adhered to the literary standard of the language. When Hole says that ' "The Voyages of Sindbad" may not unjustly be denominated the Arabian Odyssey', he was unaware of the utter contempt of al-Jahiz for أحاديث الحوائن و تزيد البحريين the stories told by wandering conjurers, and the unlikely fablings of sailor-men.' (15)

Hole is farther led astray by failing to recognise that, with development and modification at the hands of story-teller after story-teller, the *Nights* as he knew them were not a carefully-preserved reproduction of their pristine form, but contained numerous accumulations and accretions. He sets out to suggest that internal evidence shows the assumed 'author' of the *Nights* to have lived after the invasion of India and Persia by the Tartars, and to have confused these Moslem rulers with the ante-Islamic Sassanides. Hole displays a knowledge of travel books on the East, and of translations of oriental works: Renaudot's *Remarks,* his translation of *An Account of India and China by two Mohammedan Travellers,* Colonel Capper's work,(16) and Wilkin's translation of the *Heeto-pades* of Veeshnoo-Sarma, are mentioned.(17) It is notable that in *Arthur,* Hole assumes in

---

(15) كتاب الحيوان vii. 33 (Cairo, 1907). A few lines further, Jâhiz relates an anecdote similar to the story of Sindbad's adventure on the whale's back, and comments:

وهذا الحديث قد طم على الخرافات والتّهوات وحديث الخلوة

('And this species of tale fills all the fantasies and ephemeral tales, and the stories told in leisure hours').

(16) Colonel Capper, *Observations on the Passage to India,* pp. 24-5.
(17) Hole, *Remarks,* pp. 6-7 *et passim.*

his readers a greater familiarity with certain details of Moslem tradition than with the corresponding points in the newly-studied Nordic mythology. The opening of a long note ([18]) on Valhalla reads, 'The Scandinavian Valhalla, *like the Mahometan Paradise*, was supposed to have been roofed with shields. The Valkeries were employed by Odin to choose in battle those who were to perish, and like the *Houries* to wait on the selected heroes'.([19])

The main thesis of the *Remarks* is a favourable revaluation of the *Nights*. Hole considers that, although the genuineness of the work is no longer suspect, its worth is not fully appreciated; this he attempts to explain. He points to the 'national admiration' in which the work is held in Arabic-speaking countries, and compares this with its reception in Europe: he dismisses the notion that one must consider 'the Arabians, notwithstanding what we have heard of them, as children in intellect, and ourselves arrived at the maturity of knowledge' (p. 9). The translation of the *Nights* is partly to blame for this state of affairs. The version is inelegant and defective, and omits the poetical passages and reflexions with which,—so he has 'been told by gentlemen conversant in oriental literature'— the original abounds: 'What a wretched appearance would the fathers of classic poetry exhibit, if they were rendered into vulgar prose, and their most ornamental passages suppressed!' (p. 9).

The remainder of the book is devoted to rationalizing the fanciful passages in the tales. Hole's argument is based on a partial acquiescence in the view that the *Nights* cannot be appreciated by men of taste if it is considered that they contain too much that is impossible to reconcile with truth: this is an awkward position to argue from, for it is questionable whether there is much to praise in the *Arabian Nights* if this premise is accepted. But, Hole asserts, though 'the world in general is inclined to imagine, that the author has made an unlimited use

---

(18) *Arthur*, p. 120.
(19) Cf. Warton's identification of houries with Valkyries, which forms part of the argument in that portion of his work which I discuss below, pp. 135 ff.. (Dissertation I: vol. 1., p. xxviii of Price's ed., 1824.)

of the poetic privilege of *quidlibet audendi*' (p. 11), many of the fancies in the *Nights* are based on popular beliefs, on the tales of travellers, and on imitations of the classics. 'The same kind of *credibility* is preserved in these tales, as the Greeks attached to the *speciosa miracula* of their poets' (u.s.), therefore they deserve more consideration than they have been accorded. Concentrating upon the *Voyages of Sindbad,* Hole proceeds to point out the authentic descriptions of natural phenomena, the analogies in classical literature and mediaeval belief, and, very ingeniously, to attempt to locate the places mentioned in the voyages. (The latter conjectures are made use of to a considerable extent by Lane, in his note to the *Arabian Nights*.)

In this, Hole anticipates a study by Dr. Hussein Fawzy, The Tale of Sindbad of Old ( حديث السندباد القديم ) [20] in which a modern Arab oceanographer, with a European training, studies the historical background of the Sindbad stories, and those accounts in Arab historians and travellers' works, which throw light upon the legendary details in the tales.

Throughout Hole's book one is conscious of a firm classical background to the writer's theories and assumptions. Unlike later enthusiasts he shows no preference for mediaeval and 'oriental' arabesque or *grotesquerie* over the harmony of classical ideals. Speaking of what he terms the 'Saracenic masonry' of the *Faerie Queen,* he says, 'it constitutes a different order of poetic architecture from that of the classical Epic; and its inferiority must be allowed, though it possesses some peculiar and appropriate beauties' (p. 18).[21] A love of classical literature has clearly been a great incentive in the work: 'To follow up these wild stories to their primitive source, gratifies our curiosity: to trace the classic fables our youth delighted in, through the medium of a language totally distinct, and accommodated to the manners and customs of another distinguished race, cannot with justice be styled an irrational amusement' (pp. 219-20). Hole reiterates his desire, stated in the preface

---

(20) Cairo, 1943.

(21) Cf. Bishop Hurd's views in his *Letters on Chivalry and Romance* (1762), especially in Letter VIII.

to *Arthur,* for a new translation of the *Nights* : 'A scientific translator would not only be induced to trace many of these stories to a classic origin, but likewise to retrace some of the classic fictions to their primitive eastern derivation' (p. 221).

I have endeavoured to present Hole's *Remarks* as an example of the tendency to Assimilation. But, as may be seen, they contain much in the nature of Re-orientation, in the direction of mediaevalism and of a comparative study of the folk-tale. We are in fact witnessing, in Hole and his contemporaries, the beginnings of comparative studies, marred as yet, not only by the lack of system and documentation, but by the general failure to distinguish between formal literature and folk literature, oral and written transmission, substratum, basis, and accretion, parallel and borrowing, coincidence and influence.

The most notable example of misled zeal in the seeking of a new basis for research is the well-known notion of Thomas Warton, that the legends of mediaeval Europe have as their principal source the fancies of Eastern storytellers. Richard Price, in his Preface to the 1824 edition of the *History of English Poetry* (first published in 1774-81), gives a clear elucidation of the tendencies which led to Warton's exaggerated notions of Oriental influence. They arose 'from too confined a view of the natural limits of his subject, and too general an application of the system in detail'. [22] Warburton had—Price's reference is to the *Dissertation on the Origins of Books of Chivalry* (1742)— traced all the fiction of chivalry to the chronicles of the pseudo-Turpin, and of Geoffrey of Monmouth. This notion left many points 'totally irreconcileable with the state of the subject, both before and after the periods at which these productions obtained a circulation.' [23] So was instituted the urge to discover 'a more prolific fountain head'. The next step was the awareness that the literature of the East contained many parallels with mediaeval European poetry. Warton's theory was an attempt to account for the interconnexion of Eastern and Western legend.

---

(22) Warton, *History of English Poetry*, 1824 ed., i. 25.
(23) *Ibid*, p. 24.

Warton, seeing that the time of the Crusades was too late a date for the introduction of Eastern fiction into Europe, lays down that Moslem Spain is the main source of the legends. Warburton had already pointed the way to a general belief in an Arab source, and had himself supposed that the earliest European Romances were of Spanish origin. Convinced that the imagery and spirit of mediaeval literature are 'oriental' in cast, Warton goes on to declare that although some Scandinavian literature is too early in date to fit his hypothesis, he can explain this by the 'oriental' origin of the descendants of Odin. in point of fact, he formulated this latter notion as early as 1762 : in the 1754 edition of his *Observations on the Faery Queen*, he quotes (p. 43) Warburton's assertion that Eastern tales were introduced by Crusaders and pilgrims. In the corresponding passage of the 1762 edition (vol. I, pp. 62-4), he has inserted his theory on the origin of Scandinavian literature, and the heading *Romances* in the index, contains the fresh entry : 'New hypothesis, concerning the origin of their fictions I. 64 - 204.

By 1824, Price was able to say ([24]) of Warton's theory, 'A more extensive acquaintance with the general literature of the dark and middle ages has fully proved the fallacy of this assumption, which could only have been entertained in the infancy of the study'. There is, however, a certain amount of true orientalism in Warton's three introductory Dissertations. He is correct in assessing the part of the Arabs in the introduction of Greek learning into Europe.([25]) He points correctly to analogous details in the *Gesta Romanorum*, in *Kalilah wa Dimnah* and in *Petrus Alfonsus*.([26]) He expresses a 'suspicion' that the story of the *Hermit and the Angel* (chapter xxx of the version of the *Gesta* upon which he is commenting) is of oriental origin.([27]) Richard Hole (*Remarks*, p. 243) has, similarly, 'been assured that it is... narrated in a Persian Romance of great antiquity'.

---

(24) u.s.
(25) Ibid., in the dissertation *On the Introduction of Learning into England*. (edit. cit., i. cxv-cxx).
(26) Dissertation III, *On the Gesta Romanorum*, passim.
(27) *History*, edit. cit., i. ccvi.

## PSEUDO-ORIENTALISM IN TRANSITION : THE AGE OF *VATHEK*

The story, which is that of Parnell's *Hermit* and was used by Voltaire in *Zadig*, is that of Moses and Il-Khidr, which is told in *Surah 18* of the Koran.

Warton's extravagant statements arise from his belief that any particularly fanciful flights of the imagination must be of 'oriental' origin, and his ignorance of the fact that customs, beliefs, and attitudes of mind which he knew to exist in the Near East in his times, also existed in mediaeval Europe. 'The consequence has been an unavoidable confusion between the essence and the costume of romantic fiction, and the exclusive appropriation of the common property of mankind to a particular age and people'.[28] He builds up a multitude of falsities upon his assumptions :

> 'On the whole we may venture to affirm, that this chronicle supposed to contain the ideas of the Welsh bards, entirely consists of Arabian inventions' (edit. cit., p. xiv).

The fictions about Stonehenge are eastern, because

> 'We are told... that the giants conveyed the stones which compose this miraculous monument from the farthest coasts of Africa. Every one of these stones is supposed to be mystical, and to contain a medical virtue : an idea drawn from the medical skill of the Arabians'. (p. xvii).
>
> 'The Arabians cultivated the study of philosophy, particularly astronomy, with amazing ardour. Hence [?] arose the tradition that in King Arthur's reign, there subsisted at Caer-leon in Glamorganshire a college of two hundred philosophers, who studied astronomy and other sciences'. (p. xviii).

The chronicles of Geoffrey and Turpin are the first to mention

> 'giants, enchanters, dragons... And the reason is obvious : They were written at a time when a new and unnatural mode of thinking took place in Europe, introduced by our communication with the east'. (p. xxiii).

And so on. It is not difficult to detect the part which the *Arabian Nights* must have played in the construction of Warton's conception of eastern life and literature. In view of

---

(28) Price, in his preface to the *History*, i. 25.

the influence of Warburton's ideas upon Warton, it is ironic to note the contempt of the former for the *Arabian Nights,* as shown in his edition of Pope's correspondence.([29])

In the same year as Price's edition of Warton's *History*, appeared the Rev. Charles Swan's translation and study of the *Gesta Romanorum*. Subsequent research has confirmed the fact that many of the stories of the *Gesta* are oriental in origin, and many of Swan's remarks on this point remain valid. But the writer shares Warton's dogmatic notions as to what characteristics of a piece of writing must assign it to an eastern source:

> 'And whosoever presumes to utter my name, or rejoice in my hearing, command that his legs be immediately broken'. Another testimony of eastern origin. (ii. 284 and note)
> 'Whilst he reflected upon the path he should pursue, he beheld a naked boy running along the street, having his head anointed with oil, and bound with a napkin. The youth vociferated, "Hear, hear; pilgrims or slaves; whosoever would be washed, let him hasten to the gymnasium (ii. 246)...' Tde cuslom of anoinling the body afler balding is a well-known eastern practice: but the nudity of the boy running through the streets with a proclamation, I do not exactly understand'. (ii. 466)... 'Brachia... quorum digiti quantitatis debitam sibi assumpserant mensuram unguium fulgore non pretermisso' '...The nails, it should be remembered, are coloured in the East'. (ii. 376 and note).

In the last two examples, details of toilet, which we would think no more oriental than Roman, are considered evidence of Eastern origin: an interesting example of the particular range of information current at the time, upon classical and oriental life respectively. ([30])

During this age, the infancy of modern mediaevalism and of the study of comparative folklore, the *Nights* figure in these activities with a prominence which they were to lose when more of early European and Oriental literature had been studied.

---

(29) In a footnote to a letter from the Bishop of Rochester to Pope. It is reprinted in the 1886 ed. of *The Works of Pope,* ix. 23.

(30) It is also easier for us today to recognise that the naked boy so puzzling to Swan was an early instance of publicity by sample.

## PSEUDO-ORIENTALISM IN TRANSITION   THE AGE OF *VATHEK*

*The Gentlemen's Magazine* for 1797-9 contains some correspondence upon the *Nights*, little of which shows any orientalist background, though all show the growing interest in comparative studies.([31])

Francis Douce, as a student of early European literature, also appears interested in the *Nights* for the sake of comparison. We see this in his *Illustrations of Shakespeare and of Ancient Manners* (1807)—for example, on p. 377 of vol. ii—and in the marginalia he has pencilled into his copies, now in the Bodleian, of Hole's *Remarks* and of Jonathan Scott's *Tales, Anecdotes and Letters* (which includes a fragment of the *Nights*), published in 1800.

Thomas Keitly, in his *Tales and Popular Fictions; their Resemblance and Transmission from Country to Country* (1834; p. x), mentions Douce as one of the learned friends from whom he has received valuable aid: in his book, this scholar points out European analogues to *Sindbad, The Enchanted Horse*, and *The Two Jealous Sisters*. Douce's copy of Hole's *Remarks* was a gift to him from the author.

Both Douce and Gough were subscribers to the *Oriental Collections*. The 'Asiaticism' which the *Collections* professed to study is vague, and its delimitation none too certain. The Preface to the *Collections* is an illustration of the state of oriental scholarship at the time. Many of its statements are inaccurate, — as, for instance, the notion that Turkish is a modern form of the Scythian language. The differentiation between the various parts of the East is not clear, but the emphasis of the studies is upon the Near East.

With scholarship in this state of uncertainty, it is not unexpected that popular notions of the East should be vague. The ordinary reader's imagined idea of the Arab world can be judged from the illustrations made by contemporary artists for late eighteenth and early nineteenth century impressions of the *Nights*. The Harrison edition is particularly interesting, its illustrators being Stothard, Richard Corbould, and E.F. Burney The pictures show a strange mixture of genuinely oriental traits,

---

(31) See LXVII, pp. 540, 815, 1019 f., 1041, 1081; LXVIII, 304 f., 357, LXIX, 55, 91 f.

pseudo-oriental attempts, European details of dress and furnishing, and the usual classical touches incorporated in the formalised art of the time.

Thus Corbould adds oriental turbans to classical statuettes, and to figures of women in what appears to be fashionable dishabille. It is interesting that, writing as a mediaevalist, Douce ([32]) gives especial praise to Stothard ([33]) for his attention to accuracy of costume.

The first attempts to rewrite the *Nights* specifically for the child reader belong to these years. The *Nights* were already, of course, in their English translation, favourite reading for children, as we have seen Richard Hole regretting. But the re-writing of classics, in order to adapt them to the child reader, with a didactic end in view, seems a new development, typical of the age of Maria Edgeworth. Around 1790 ([34]) appeared *The Oriental Moralist: or the Beauties of the Arabian Nights Entertainments Translated from the original and accompanied with suitable reflexions adapted to each Story*, by the Rev'd. Mr. [J.] Cooper. This was not his first venture in moral works for the young:[35] in this adaptation he does not hesitate to follow a plan he outlines in the preface (pp. 3-4), of expurging passages, and adding reflexions, and he has even 'in many instances considerably altered the fables,' to give them a turn which appeared... the most likely to promote the love of virtue.'

The expurging follows the lines one might expect: the Third Calendar's relations with the forty beautiful ladies in the enchanted castle turn from those of rotational concubinage to those of idyllic comradeship; where impropriety cannot be eliminated, it is reduced: the crime of the First Calendar's

---

(32) *Op. cit.*, ii. 284 and note.

(33) The same illustrator of whom Charles Lamb writes (in his poem *To T. Stothard* Esq., first published in *The Athenaeum*, Dec. 21, 1833):
'In my young days
How often have I with a child's fond gaze
Pored on the pictured wonders thou hadst done'.

(34) In manuscript on the fly-leaf of the British Museum copy of Cooper's *Moralist* is the note 'New Book/1793'.

(35) Cooper, *op. cit.*, preface, p. 4.

cousin is here adultery instead of incest, — an alteration also to be made by Edward Lane.

I have not seen the anonymous *Beauties of the Arabian Nights* (1792) (³⁶), but the 1808 *Beauties of the Arabian Nights Entertainments* follows Cooper's principles. (³⁷)

Another abridged version is the *Arabian Nights Entertainments... Freely Transcribed from the Original Translation, Printed for C.D. Piguenit*, 1792. Piguenit approached the book as a bookseller who has 'devoted his attention... for the greater part of the past twenty years to the service of schools', and quotes in support of his project the opinion of Vicesimus Knox in favour of the *Nights* as a kindler of the flame of *genius* in boys.(³⁸) Piguenit's version retells the tales in too cursory a manner, in the style of the anecdote.

His moralistic alteration are sometimes inept if one has in mind the details of the original. Piguenit will not allow Dinarzade to pass the night in the same room as the married couple ; Scheherezade having requested that she might see her in the morning, 'an hour before day, at the appointed hour, Dinarzade was admitted into the nuptual chamber' (i. 17). In the *Three Calendars*, the porter is not given permission by the ladies to spend the night in their home, but only 'to continue till evening' (i. 64). Not even is the unfortunate youth in the *Third Calender* permitted to be bathed and dried by his companion Prince Agib ; simply 'being fatigued' he lies down to repose (i. 112), — thus the tragic irony of his accidental death at Agib's hand is impaired.

In his preface, Piguenit shows a noteworthy distaste for wonder. He hopes the changes 'will be found to have been in favour of probability or of good morals'. Physical and social

---

(36) Mentioned by Chauvin, *Bibliothèque des ouvrages arabes*, 1892-1922; iv. 70, n. 2.

(37) It is unlikely to be a verbatim reprint of the 1792 *Beauties*, for the preface is that of a first edition: 'If this Volume is favourably received,' it reads, 'a second volume, (which is now in a state of forwardness) will be published, containing, "The Beauties of the Continuation to the Arabian Nights".'

(38) *Essays Moral and Literary*, enlarged edition,, 1782; i. 314.

improbabilities, psychological inconsistencies, inexplicable behaviour, even magic, are reduced to a neo-classical rationality, sometimes by adding an explanation. To reconcile Schahriar's deeds with moral standards and to give consistency to his character, we are told, 'This prince, though hasty and violent in his temper, had many virtues' (i.1). Amine's visitor, an old woman whom she has never met before, becomes 'a venerable lady, whom I had noticed at the public baths' (i.133). The following passages are typical contrasts:

| *The 1708 translation of Galland:* | *Piguenit:* |
|---|---|
| 'She presented me with a cup full of such water as I was accustomed to drink; but instead of putting it to my mouth, I went to a window that stood open, and threw out the water so privately, that she did not perceive it, and put the cup again into her hands, to persuade her that I had drank it'. (1789 ed., i. 73) | 'When she presented me, before we retired, with a cup, I only pretended to drink, and holding it to my mouth sometime, I returned it to her untasted:' |
| 'This being done, the *sea* will swell and *rise up* to the foot of the dome that stands upon the top of the mountain' (i. 1953.) | 'This being done, the *mountain* will gradually sink *down* into the sea. (i. 107-8.) |

That there were earlier 'abstracts' of the *Nights* is suggested by Wordsworth's reference (*Prelude*, V, 461-2) to

    A little, yellow canvas-cover'd Book,
    A slender abstract of the Arabian Tales,

which he possessed as a nine-year old child. We are still as unable to identify this edition as Livingston Lowes was in 1927 ([39]); for Wordsworth to have had this book in his hands at the age of nine it must have appeared at the latest in 1779, earlier than the texts we have glanced at. ([40])

---

(39) *The Road to Xanadu;* 1930 ed., note on pp. 459-61.
(40) And earlier than the *Novelists' Magazine* edition of 1785.

Again in contrast with the general acceptance throughout the earlier period, of the sometimes highly inadequate text of the English translation made of Galland's *Nights* for the publisher Bell in 1708, the turn of the century sees some attempts at revising the *Nights* in order to make the English version more correct and more elegant, and to supply it with notes based on passages in orientalist sources, to add authenticity and scholarly interest to them. The 1798 Edinburgh revision, published anonymously, is attributed by John Nichols [41] to Richard Gough. This edition is the first to contain a preface of any length, and shows evidence of collation with the French, correcting errors of translation and making emendations suggested by common sense. These emendations being those of a conscientious and intelligent collator, but not an orientalist, they are not always correct. In the story of *The Grecian King* a game of polo is called *melle* by Galland, and *mell* by Bell's translator. The physician recommends the king to mount his horse and play at the game. Gough can see the absurdity of playing *croquet* on horseback. He modifies the text, so that the King is asked to 'take horse, and go to the place where he used to play at melle' (i. 49); a bland footnote reads, 'In the French, this game is played on horseback.' The Rev. Edward Forster retranslated Galland in 1802, again referring to recent and contemporary authorities, and showing a care for authenticity which, excepting for the fact that Forster himself knew no Arabic, is a case in which Miss Conant's remark quoted above is more justifiable than it is when applied to other works. Beaumont's inadequate revision of 1811 does not live up to its claims (in its *Advertisement*) to rescue the *Nights* from bad writing, indecency, and incompleteness.

The opening of the nineteenth century saw the maturing of the most notable of the non-orientalist movements in which the translations of Arabic imaginative literature became involved. This is, of course, the Romantic movement. [42] Much

---

(41) *Literary Anecdotes*, (1812-15); vi. 318.
(42) Compare, and contrast, with these pages, Monsieur Parreaux' analyses in his caps, vi and vii.

conjecture can be made as to the reasons why the Orient was adopted by the Romantic writers as one of their favourite themes. The question cannot be answered by any simple and clear-cut assertion. It is bound up with the general problem of the rise of Romanticism, over which even more conjecture can, and has, been made.

Armand Abel ([43]) points out that the tales of the *Arabian Nights* were collected chiefly for the enjoyment of the bourgeoisie of the Arab world in the later Middle Ages, at which time the comfortable but dull life of the merchant classes had become one of the features of Islamic social structure. Bearing this in mind, one might be inclined to link the popularity of the oriental tale in the early nineteenth century with the sociological theories which have been suggested in explanation of the growth of the Romantic movement. This notion may partially explain the popularity of the pseudo-oriental poetry which appeared at the time : but it is insufficient for further purposes. As an interpretation of the general change of outlook it takes no account of the existence in the second half of the eighteenth century of the very different bourgeois-inspired domestic novel ; nor can it be a conclusive explanation of an orientalist cult in which there figure such aristocrats as Beckford and Byron.

It is clear, however, that around 1800, imaginative writers began to make use of the pseudo-Orient in a fresh manner. The didactic possibilities of the subject in the prose essay and in fiction were all but exhausted. A widening in the range of subjects and styles considered suitable for poetry was taking place : and the oriental tale was one of the themes which were affected by this broadening. There were probably a number of fortuitous elements which contributed to the oriental vogue. Contemporary political events brought Egypt, Greece, Turkey, and the Levant into prominence. Travels and archeological studies had the same effect. Writers made use of stories which appealed to them through their plot, but which, being of

---

(43) *Les Enseignements des Mille et une Nuits*, p. 156, Brussels, 1939.

oriental origin, made an orientalizing treatment of them adviseable.(⁴⁴)

Further than this, three elements of the Romantic spirit, I believe, gave the tendency its full strength : the desire to escape into a world rather different from the writer's own, the desire to create one's own subjective world, and the love of picturesque local colour.

The importance of any of these tendencies, on its own, should not be exaggerated. The notion of complete escape from the familiar is an unsatisfactory explanation of the movement. The poets did not turn to the entirely unfamiliar—to China or the Antipodes— but to the half-known, to a world which seemed different enough to be attractive, but similar enough to be appreciated by their own scale of values.(⁴⁵) The Near East was connected with their lives by their childhood reading, by its relationship to the classical and Biblical worlds which were the background of their education, by the contemporary accounts of warfare, travels, and discovery. (This assertion needs some qualification, for the Near East does on occasion figure in a purely negative role in Romantic literature that does not deal specifically with it. It is, for example, the undefined, distant, land to which Crusaders and pilgrims go, leaving behind them the women and kinsmen with whose life during the period of separation a poem is concerned). It is represented as the source of the driving-forces of paganism, tyranny or ignorance, in tales where it is required that the symbolic antithesis of an underlying ideal should be sketched in, and identified with something recognizable to the reader : the ideal in question may

---

(44) But contrast Parnell's treatment of the *Hermit*, mentioned above, p. 125 note and p. 137.

(45) 'Not only on the fascinating fringes of early maps, but universally, the advancing territory of the known is rimmed and bounded by a dubious borderland in which the unfamiliar and the strange hold momentary sway. And that zone of the marvellous (which is merely the unknown in its transition to the wonted) draws like a loadstone the incorporating energy of the imagination, which penetrates to the core of the familiar behind the outward semblance of the strange, and completes the conquest which discovery began'. Livingstone Lowes, *The Road to Xanadu* (revised ed., p. 115).

vary from Christianity to what Brandes (⁴⁶) calls 'radical naturalism'.

The erudition involved in the depicting of local colour is sometimes overstressed. Wallace C. Brown's article on *Byron and English Interest in the Near East* (*Studies in Philology*, xxxiv, 1937, pp. 55 ff.) stresses the relationship between the poetic vogue, and contemporary knowledge of the region.(⁴⁷) Both scholars and travellers were bringing the 'glamorous reality' of the East nearer to the English public, and so stimulated the interest of imaginative writers. In essence, this is undeniably true, but Mr. Brown's assertion that the taste of the early nineteenth century required more accurate accounts of travels than that of the previous age, is open to some question. He quotes as an illustration of the new tendency, an extract from the *Eclectic Review* of 1817, which appears to me to exemplify, rather, the very essence of the eighteenth century : describing the interest in travel, the *Review* calls it 'an interest we do not say partaking strongly of the poetical or enthusiastic, —but which, though of a calmer tone, is sustained in the writer by so advantageous a combination of taste, intelligence, and knowledge, that it draws the reader on with vivacity in some parts, and without sense of weariness in all'. Again, Mr. Brown quotes the Review as saying, in 1812, of Near Eastern lands, of these countries... our information is singularly minute and 'copious' : this he gives as evidence of the thoroughness of contemporary studies, but since we know how inadequate they were, the remark is surely confirmation of the comparatively low standards of erudition in this field ? Howard Mumford Jones (⁴⁸) suggests that among the causes of the decline of interest in the Romantic poets must rank their excessive bookishness, one of the manifestations of which is their numerous

---

(46) *Main Currents in Nineteenth Century Literature,* English version, 1906, vol. iv: *Naturalism in England*, p. 207 et passim.

(47) I have not seen the same author's dissertation *The Near East as Theme and Background in English Literature 1775-1825, with Special Emphasis on the Literature of Travel*, University of Michigan, 1934.

(48) *The Harp that Once — A Chronicle of the Life of Thomas Moore*, New York, 1937

and tiresome footnotes. But to study the poetry in favour at the present day involves far more delving into notes, sources, and biographical material, and most readers of the Romantic poets would, in any case, either omit the notes, or use editions which do not reproduce them. It is true that a love of picturesque detail, and a certain pose of showmanship, characterize many of the Romantics,—both when the exhibits are of their own creation, as, at one end of the era, *Vathek* is, and when they are exotic scenes being freshly portrayed as in Lane's *Modern Egyptians,* at the other extreme in date and in approach. But the poets did not hesitate to ignore or contradict the factual accounts upon which their work was based: the interests of erudition were certainly subordinated to those of art.

The pseudo-Orient thus offered a new field for self-projection; it offered fresh themes, it provided a useful background for satire or self-exhibition. It suggested all the attraction and potentiality of half-knowledge; linked with the Middle Ages by many similarities of outlook, it was further linked with them in the imaginative writers' minds, for escape and self-projection into a distant land was a pleasant variant of escape and self-projection into the Past.

One must mention, in addition, the erotic appeal of the East to western imagination. This had existed for several centuries, but Romanticism, by its nature and the range of its topics, gave new life to the theme. No overt statement of this attraction appears to have been made in any contemporaneous work of criticism: its influence, however, is clear.

An example of the combination of the various elements which gave attraction to the East,—ranging from Biblical interest to romantic escapism, is afforded by Thomas Keitley's remarks [49] on the *Arabian Nights*: the passage is worth quoting at some length:

> It is needless to ask whence the charms of these tales arise: the wonderful will alway have attractions, brilliant imagination will always assert its power, and the circumstance of our religion, and the volume in which it is

---

(49) *Op. cit.,* pp. 32-3.

contained, being derived from the East, raises in the youthful mind an early predilection for that part of the world. The East, we are taught, contained the blissful Paradise of man's infancy and innocence, which the genius of Milton has filled with all that can yield delight... The East... was, in fact, the land of miracle and wonder, favoured with the choicest regards of the Deity; and imagination has always invested its front with a nimbus of splendour. Such, at least, were my own early impressions of the East; and I should suppose that I am but one of the many. The Thousand and One Nights and similar collections, come to augment this illusion; the noble Vision of Mirza and other fictions of the same kind lend their aid; and I apprehend there are few persons fond of reading who have not exaggerated ideas of the magnificence and beauty of that part of the world lurking in the recesses of their imagination. Nor is this illusion (as those who have lost it well know), to be deplored. Many are the dark and cloudy days of life; and most happy is he for whom they are most frequently gilded by the rays of fancy. And the brilliant fictions of the East, and the popular tales which amused our childhood, and still recall its pleasures, have in this the advantage over the modern novel—they go at once beyond the regions of probability, and cannot therefore injure by exciting romantic expectations of the fortune of the hero or heroine being realised in ourselves.

A good many of the Romantic tendencies here sketched arise only in the opening years of the nineteenth century. Others, however, are already to be found in Beckford's *Vathek*. Beckford's orientalism is certainly not the old didactic orientalism of say, Addison's *Mirza*; it is a complete escape from his own environment, it creates a totally subjective world, indeed, almost a private mythology; it shows a certain interest, at the same time, in eastern local colour, and, with Henley's copious notes based on D'Herbelot, William Jones, and other orientalists, to illustrate features which Beckford has incorporated into his creative fiction, it anticipates Moore and Southey.

A traveller like most of his Romantic successors, he had studied Arabic, had apparently translated freely from Arabic MSS and had lived in the dream world of an Orient evoked by his reading of other travellers. *Vathek*'s implied message of anti-moralism, its pleased interest in the egotistic, and in the near-satanic, its descriptive passages, its powerful and ambiguous close, class it with the verse tales of the Romantics.

It is, nevertheless, the last, the culminating rococo prose tale of the pseudo-Orient, resembling in this the work of Cazotte, that belated continuator of the Galland tradition. It delights in *turqueries*, in comic monstrosities of cruelty, gluttony and lust, in the spirit of the libretti of *Così Fan Tutte* or of *Il Seraglio*, a spirit which *Vathek* itself perhaps helped to pass on to Byron, to Meredith and beyond. Like Hamilton, he satirizes the genre he employs. He shares with the eighteenth-century *philosophe*, rather than with the Romantic enthusiast, the impish cock-snooking at clericalism, the success in conveying the tediousness of the religiose. Beckford on occasion is Gibbonian even in style :

> His wives... incessantly supplied him with prayers for his health, and water for his thirst.[50]

In all these respects, Beckford looks back to the *Nights* tradition, and had his rightful place in Miss Conant's galaxy.

By the very fact that *Vathek* belongs to both these two major phases, it is transitional in status. But, in addition, it can be seen to belong specifically to that intermediary trend, or bundle of trends, marking the last quarter of the eighteenth-century, to which this paper has been mainly devoted. It shares with the children's adapters, with the re-writers of the *Nights,* with the scholars who made oblique use of orientalism, some of the features of this phase. Thus, all radiated out upon new ground, outside the main trends of, roughly, 1708 to around 1774. It 're-orientates' attention, or attempts to, in connexion with morality, conventional behaviour, imaginative ability, and aesthetics. Even with the children's adapters, it has this further point in common : that both adapt a heritage, they towards greater propriety and morality, he towards a latent philosophy, or lesson, of *immoralisme*. Beckford is thus the obverse of Piguenit and Cooper, and all have moved, each in his fashion, away from the main eighteenth-century stock acceptances. With the academic students of romance, the

---

(50) P. 203 of the Everyman ed.

similarity of interest is clearer; the text of *Vathek* (Henley's notes seeming to emphasize this) reveals the creative writer's equivalent of the scholar's interest in the fragmentary data out of which an imaginative reconstruction of a pattern of life may be made.

Beckford's genius is, let us grant, a minor one, but it is not a constricted one. This essay cannot branch away from the discussion of period affinities to a more general estimate of the merits of Beckford's writings, but even within the bounds of the present theme, *Vathek* draws one to the very edge. For, besides his affinities to his own age, to his immediate predecessors and his immediate successors, Beckford looks forward, as Byron does among those nearer to him in time, to a much later line of sophisticated wit-writers, to Wilde, Firbank, and Mr. Evelyn Waugh. At the same time, he anticipates, and, without doubt, influences, the *Shaving of Shagpat,* and also has very much in common (perhaps again through direct influence?) with the fantasy, at once impish and limpid, of James Branch Cabell. How many other minor writers can be studied from so many different angles, and have so many different threads attached to them, and survive the scholarly and critical hug with such evident spiritedness?

CELEBRATION OF THE BICENTENARY

OF THE BIRTH OF

WILLIAM BECKFORD

1760–1844

AUTHOR, COLLECTOR, ECCENTRIC

*Invitation to Beckford Bicentenary Exhibition, 12th October, 1960.*

*William Beckford of Fonthill* / WRITER, TRAVELLER, COLLECTER, CALIPH / 1760-1844 / A BRIEF NARRATIVE AND CATALOGUE OF / AN EXHIBITION TO MARK THE TWO HUNDREDTH / ANNIVERSARY OF BECFORD'S BIRTH / *by Howard B. Gotlieb* / WITH THE PREVIOUSLY UNPUBLISHED JOURNAL / KEPT BY WILLIAM BECKFORD IN 1794 / *Edited by Boyd Alexander* / YALE UNIVERSITY LIBRARY / *New Haven, Connecticut* / 1960.

Examining the catalogue of the Beckford Exhibition at Yale, (received through the kindness of Mr. James T. Babb, Yale Librarian and Beckford Collector) is, fortunately, second best to viewing the exhibition itself.

The *Catalogue* cites 257 items of varied interest and value, classified under six heads :

1. William Beckford, Sr., Lord Mayor of London.
2. The Life and Works of William Beckford.
3. Books attributed to William Beckford.
4. Beckford as the Caliph of Fonthill Abbey.
5. Beckford the Collector.
6. Books about William Beckford.

One cannot judge of the arrangement of the exhibition [1] from reading the *Catalogue* but one can at least judge of the value of the items exhibited. It is rich indeed in autograph letters by and about William Beckford and in first editions (and virtually every edition) of his works.

The second is naturally of most interest and value to many Beckford scholars, including as it does, such valued items as the famous "Chavannes" copy of *Vathek* (item 25) and Beckford's

---

[1] See *The Times Literary Supplement*, October 28, 1960, p. 699 for an account of the exhibition.

letter to Henley, Feb. 9, 1786, forbidding the publication of *Vathek* for another year (item 19).

Brief but fairly adequate exposition of the importance of particular items, together with ample quotations from autograph letters qualify this *Catalogue* to stand on the reference shelf next to Guy Chapman's *Bibliography of William Beckford,* for which purpose it should seem the *Catalogue* was partly designed.

The last section (Books abut William Beckford) should be of great help to any new recruits to Beckford studies. It is however the poorest and least exhaustive of all sections of the *Catalogue*.

The work of André Parreaux who has been a devoted Beckfordian for more than thirty years should have been more fully represented. His two papers on Beckford and Byron (*Etudes Anglaises,* Paris, 1956), should have been included, together with a more recent publication "Beckford en Italie", published by the *Revue de Littérature Comparée,* Paris, (1960 ?). Another ommission is Schaverell Sitwell's curious *Beckford and Beckfordism* (London, Duckworth, 1930). A work which one might include in this section is a PH.D. thesis on the shelves of Yale Library. It is Harold S.L. Wiener's *The Eastern Backgroudn of Byron's Turkish Tales* (1938), where the inflence of *Vathek* on Byron's *Turkish Tales* is studied in great detail.

Beckford the Collector was well represented in the exhibition and this section is probably the most interesting from the point of view of the *bibliophile*. This large section is cleverly rounded by the inclusion of the catalogues of the three great sales of Beckford's books (1808, 1823 ané 1882-3). One can only hope that the more fortunate mortals who could view the exhibition were duly impressed by the extent of the eccentric millionnaire's aquisitiveness and the pungency of the notes he savagely jotted down in his priceless copies.

Mr. Boyd Alexander has contributed two valuable Appendices to the *Catalogue*. Appendix I (pp. 83-5) is a statement concerning the authorship of *Al Raoui,* which he thinks was the work of William Beckford. The statement attempts to answer the six arguments put forward by Guy Chapman in his letter to the *Times Literary Supplement* (October 31, 1936) ([2]) :

1) He presumes that Mrs. Cuthbert to whom the books was dedicated, must have been the wife of Mrs. Hervey's Jamaican attorney, "mentioned in Pedley's letter to Beckford, dated 17 december 1802".

It seems rather farfetched, however, that Beckford should dedicate a book to the wife of his sister's Jamaican attorney when we have no evidence that he ever met a lady of that name. Mr. Alexander adds that, *"in manuscript* the work is not dedicated to anyone".

2) He casts some doubt on Henley's authorship of the poems published in the same volume as *Al Raoui,* but in the absence of any evidence of Beckford's authorship, one is more inclined to believe Nichols' *Illustration of the Literary History of the Eighteenth Century* (1858) which attributes them to Henley. Mr. B. Alexander states that no poems are attached to the manuscript of *Al Raoui.*

3) He attempts to refute Chapman's argument that the story of *Al Raoui,* is mentioned in the *Notes* of *Vathek* written by Henley by reminding us that :

> ....both men collaborated in the *Notes,* which were prepared under Beckford's supervision.... If Beckford translated *Al Raoui* from the Arabic in 1783 (intending to publish it soon after writing *Vathek,* the mention of it in the *Notes* to *Vathek,* published in 1786, would not be surprising.

The note, however, to which both Chapman and Alexander refer could not possibly have been written by Beckford, nor prepared under his supervision. It refers to *Al-Raoui* as "Translated from one of the unpublished manuscripts mentioned in the preface".([3]) Obviously this is a reference to a passage in the preface in which Henley alleged that *Vathek* was a translation of one of the Wortley Montagu MSS :

---

([2]) cf, *supra,* 104-108.
([3]) *An Arabian Tale* (1786), p. 279.

> The Original of the following story, with some others of a similar kind, collected in the East by a Man of Letters, was communicated to the Editor above three years ago. The pleasure he received from the perusal of it, induced him at that tim to transcribe and since to translate it.... ([4])

As Henley was the writer of the preface which robbed the young millionnaire of the glory of the authorship of the *Arabian Tale,* one must conclude that he also wrote the note refering to the preface. It does not follow, however, that Henley was the *translator* of the little tale. It may have been translated into French by Beckford when he was working under Zemir. Henley was asked (or volunteered) to translate the French version into English and Mme de Starck made a fair copy of the translation. Whether Henley kept the rough copy, or had another fair copy at his disposal is immaterial for in any case he had access to Beckford's papers when he was working on the translation of *Vathek.* When he finally decided to take advantage of Beckford's absence on the Continent, he probably had the intention of following the publication of the *Arabian Tale* with the publication of *Al Raoui* and other translations from the Wortley Montagu MSS.

Beckford's strong reaction over the affair of *Vathek* put an end to any project of the sort. In spite of his self enforced exile, the young millionnaire was not as impotent as the impecunious clergyman had speculated; he was still powerful in hired henchmen in the form of solicitors, bankers and agents of every type.

The lapse of some twelve years and the publication of Scotts' translation in Ouseley's *Oriental Collections* (1798), may have encouraged the clergyman (always in search for patronage) to put forth part of his early project. The tale was too slight to fill a volume of even the smallest size and so the poems were thrown in as further evidence of the exceptional literary abilities of the editor-poet.

---

(4) *ibid,* preface, iii.

Mr. Alexander's statement that the manuscript of *Al Raoui* in the Beckford papers has no dedication and is not attached to any poems would further support this hypothesis.

4) Mr. Alexander dismisses the evidence of Jonathan Scott as worthless since he must have derived his information from Henley himself who was the principal of Haileybury College 1805-1815.

Dismissing J. Scott's note on the grounds of Henley's "shiftiness and treachery" cannot here be regarded as conclusive and would not exclude the possibility of Henley being resposible for the publication if not for the translation of *Al Raoui*, nor do *No.s* 5 and 6 exclude the same possibility.(5)

After this attempt to answer Guy Chapman's arguments, Mr. Alexander makes some points of his own to support Beckford's authorship (Mr. Alexander does not commit himself on the point of the *publication* of the tale). One of these points is that:

> There is in the Papers an unpublished *Suite* to *Al Raoui*, written out by the same copyist who transcribed the French version of *Al Raoui*. This amusing and inproper *Suite* is unquestionably Beckford's composition;

Dr. André Parreaux gives a summary of this same *Suite* (6), which shows that it is mainly a translation from the same MSS as *Al Raoui*. In the catalogue of the Wortley Montagu MSS printed in R.F. Burton's *Supplemental Nights*, V (498-504). "The Courtier's Story.... (the original of *Al Raoui*)" is followed

---

(5) Mr. B. Alexander answers Chapman's fifth point (cf. *supra*, 106) by the statement, "But in Beckford's Papers there are other Oriental Tales only in fair-copy which are not in Beckford's hand and which do not in every case have his emendations ; he was too indolent to make extensive fair-copies himself, and often destroyed the originals from which they were made"

To the argument that there is no copy of *Al Raoui* in the Hamilton Palace Sale Catalogue he answers that "...it is entered in the manuscript *Catalogue of the Easton Park Library* (now at Brodick Castle), in which several of his other rare works appear, as well as a number of books from his library with his notes in."

(6) Parreaux, André. *William Beckford, Auteur de* Vathek (1760-1844)..., A.G. Nizet, Paris, 1960, pp. 142-5.

by "Another relation of the Courtier, Night cdcxi". A note between brackets (probably by Burton) runs, "(*Here Iblis took the place of a musician.*) (⁷)

In Burton's translation of the *Nights*, the same story appears in two versions: first as "Ibrahim of Mosul and the devil",(⁸) where the devil appears before the great musician of Al Rashid in the guise of an old musician. It is followed by the story of "The Lovers of the Banu Uzrah" (⁹) which is another version of the story translated in *Al Raoui*. The second version is more closely related to the *Suite* in the Beckford Papers. It is the story of "Ishak of Mosul and his Mistress and the devil".(¹⁰)

One must conclude that both *Al Raoui* and the *Suite* were translations, probably by Beckford during the period of his work under Zemir's tutorship.*

The second Appendix contributed by Mr. Alexander is a more valuable addition to Beckfordian scholarship. It is Beckford's 1794 Journal which he used forty years later as the basis of his *Recollections of an Excursion to the Monasteries of Alcobaça and Batalha* (1935).

Beckford was apparently flattered by the success of *Italy, with Sketches of Spain and Portugal* (1834) and his publisher was encouraged to venture the publication of author travel by the same author. Beckford rummaged his old papers for these

---

(7) Burton, R.F. *Supplemental Nights...*, (1888), V, p. 501.

(8) Burton, R.F. *The Book of the Thousand Nights and a Night*, VII, pp. 113-6.

(9) *ibid*, 117-124.

(10) *ibid*, 136-9.

\* *The Times Literary Supplement* of November 25, 1960 received at the time of publication has published a letter from Guy Chapman (p. 759), which seconds our conclusions. Of Mr. Alexander's answers he says: "...they do not meet the principal objection that there is no serious material evidence for Beckford having any hand in the 1799 publication; that he never mentioned, let alone acknowledged, the book; and that the first attribution occurs after his death in Redding's biography in which not a relevant word from Beckford is quoted."

scraps of a Journal now published for the first time by Mr. Alexander. It consists of "twelve pages of text on four different type of writing material."

Though some readers may not agree with Mr. Alexander that the Journal is stylistically superior to the book, it is nevertheless a most interesting discovery and we are all greatly indebted to him for editing it.

F. M. M.

## OUR CONTRIBUTORS

BOYD ALEXANDER: M.A. Oxon, Custodian of the Beckford Papers.

GEOFFREY BULLOUGH: Professor of English at King's College in the University of London.

FATMA MOUSSA MAHMOUD: Lecturer in English at the Faculty of Arts in the University of Cairo.

MAHMOUD MANZALAOUI: Lecturer in English at the Faculty of Arts in the University of Alexandria.

ANDRE PARREAUX: Professor of English at the University of Lille (France).

MAGDI WAHBA: Lecturer in English at the Faculty of Arts in the University of Cairo.